→ INTRODUCING

MODERNISM

CHRIS RODRIGUES & CHRIS GARRATT

Published in the UK in 2010
by Icon Books Ltd.,
Omnibus Business Centre,
39-41 North Road, London N7 9DP
email: info@iconbooks.co.uk
www.introducingbooks.com

This edition published in the USA
in 2010 by Totem Books
Inquiries to: Icon Books Ltd.,
Omnibus Business Centre,
39-41 North Road,
London N7 9DP, UK

Sold in the UK, Europe, South Africa
and Asia by Faber and Faber Ltd.,
Bloomsbury House,
74-77 Great Russell Street,
London WC1B 3DA
or their agents

Distributed to the trade in the USA
by National Book Network Inc.,
4501 Forbes Boulevard, Suite 200,
Lanham, Maryland 20706

Distributed in the UK, Europe,
South Africa and Asia by TBS Ltd.,
TBS Distribution Centre,
Colchester Road, Frating Green,
Colchester CO7 7DW

Distributed in Canada by
Penguin Books Canada,
90 Eglinton Avenue East, Suite 700
Toronto, Ontario M4P 2Y3

ISBN: 978-184831-116-9

This edition published in Australia
in 2010 by Allen & Unwin Pty. Ltd.,
PO Box 8500, 83 Alexander Street,
Crows Nest, NSW 2065

Previously published in 2001

Originating editor: Richard Appignanesi

Printed by Gutenberg Press, Malta

Realizing Modernism

This book will try to answer 15 basic questions on modernism, and is specifically concerned with modernism in the arts.

1. What is modernism?

2. When does modernism begin?

3. What is the difference between modernism and "modernity"?

4. Is modernism just a reaction to modernity?

5. How do we recognize a "modernist" work?

6. Is there a modernist theory in relation to practice?

7. What is the relation of modernism to primitivism?

8. What is the relation of modernism to psychoanalysis?

9. What is the role of the city in modernism?

10. Why are modernists so often "exiles"?

11. What is the role of élites and avant-gardes in modernism?

12. What politics did modernists espouse?

13. How does modernism relate to mass culture?

14. What is the relation of cinema to modernism?

15. Has modernism ended?

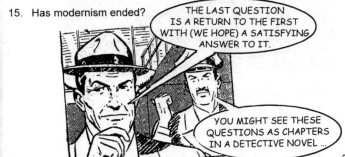

THE LAST QUESTION IS A RETURN TO THE FIRST WITH (WE HOPE) A SATISFYING ANSWER TO IT.

YOU MIGHT SEE THESE QUESTIONS AS CHAPTERS IN A DETECTIVE NOVEL ...

What is Modernism?

What is the first feature of modernism that is generally acknowledged? Most of us will agree that a modernist work is perceived as difficult, and that its difficulty is associated with unfamiliarity and difference. **D.H. Lawrence** (1885–1930), who might himself be classified a modernist writer, expressed this feeling of the pleasure and pain of difficulty.

"… to read a really new novel will always hurt, to some extent. There will always be resistance. The same with new pictures, new music. You may judge of their reality by the fact that they do arouse a certain resistance, and compel, at length, a certain acquiescence."

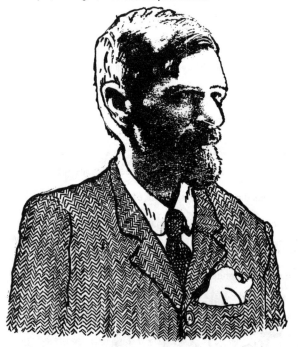

All works that can be accommodated under the umbrella of modernism – or, as we'll see, schools of **modernisms** – share a relationship to the modern world which is peculiarly new and exceptional to any other previous cultural and historical condition.

Novelty and difficulty form a special *historical* alliance. That's one feature. Another is the reply that most people will give to the question: "What is modernism?" More than likely, they will identify it by *naming* its icons.

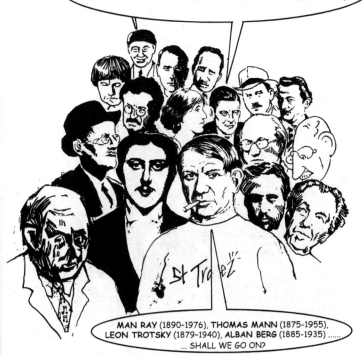

> PABLO PICASSO (1881-1973), SALVADOR DALÍ (1904-89), T.S. ELIOT (1888-1965), ARNOLD SCHOENBERG (1874-1951), LE CORBUSIER (1887-1965), KASIMIR MALEVICH (1878-1935).

> ... EZRA POUND (1885-1972), FRANK LLOYD WRIGHT (1867-1959), MARCEL PROUST (1871-1922), VIRGINIA WOOLF (1882-1941), IGOR STRAVINSKY (1882-1971), RAINER MARIA RILKE (1875-1926) ...

> MAN RAY (1890-1976), THOMAS MANN (1875-1955), LEON TROTSKY (1879-1940), ALBAN BERG (1885-1935) ......
> ... SHALL WE GO ON?

Interesting reasons can be found – positive and negative – why these names occur. Let's consider just three from this list.

Media High Profile

What makes an icon? Picasso is likely to be remembered not just because he was a "great artist". Media notoriety is crucial.

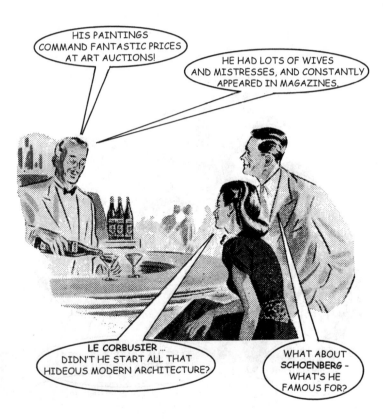

Arnold Schoenberg might not figure so high in the media stakes. His brand of ("classical"?) modernist music is, of all the modernisms, the most élitist and remote from the feelings of contemporary society. What does the "a-tonal" style or the "serial" system of composition mean to us? Most of us are happier with less cerebral forms of music that we can still identify as modern.

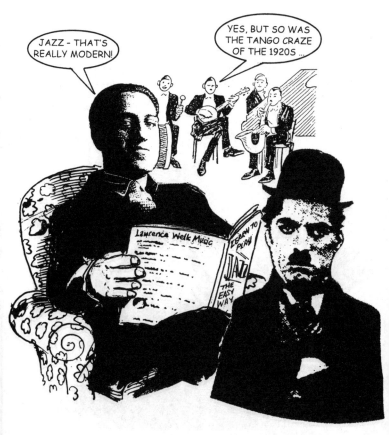

Is **George Gershwin** (1898–1937) modern? Is **Charlie Chaplin** (1899–1977) modernist? We risk confusing modernism with mainstream fashions.

Keeping up with Fashion

Fashion has the benefit of making us reflect on what modernism *isn't*, what it was *reacting against*, what it intended to *replace*.

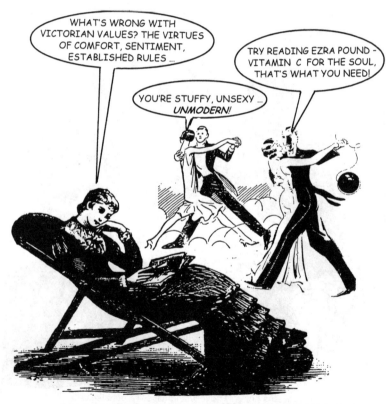

And this might lead us to think of trends or movements characteristic of modernism – for instance, Cubism, Dadaism or Surrealism – instead of simply naming personalities.

Such **isms** – indeed moder**nism** itself – provide clues to the "spirit of the age", the *Zeitgeist* as it's often called. Modernism expresses the new energies sweeping through from the late 19th century onwards – the revolutionary potentials opened up by Marx, Freud, Nietzsche and others.

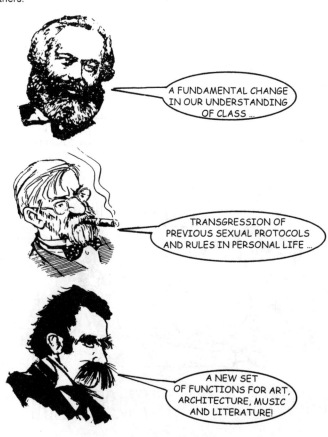

A FUNDAMENTAL CHANGE IN OUR UNDERSTANDING OF CLASS ...

TRANSGRESSION OF PREVIOUS SEXUAL PROTOCOLS AND RULES IN PERSONAL LIFE ...

A NEW SET OF FUNCTIONS FOR ART, ARCHITECTURE, MUSIC AND LITERATURE!

So, modernism concerns not only novelty and difficulty, but also a change in social dynamics. Nevertheless, we are still in the realm of generalities. How do we identify the *specifics* of modernism? Perhaps the question of modernism's **timeliness** is a good way to begin.

Chronologies and dates are often seen as the boring bits of cultural history. Stuff we glance at, or skip over, in our hurry to get to the "heart of the matter". But with accounts of modernism, something strange happens. Dates and starting points begin to matter. The problem with defining modernism is that of fixing a chronology – who did what *first*, *when* and *where*? Establishing the credentials of **originality** is crucial to modernism.

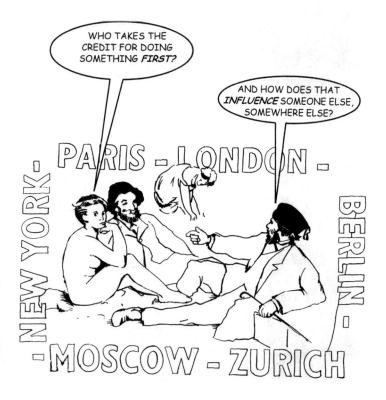

We can get lost in a complex schedule of "originalities" that pollinate each other across frontiers – but always from one major city to another: Paris, London, Berlin, Moscow, Zurich, New York …

Modernism appears like an international conspiracy, a wildfire contagion, an irresistible epidemic. But this can make us forget how limited it was to small, so-called "avant-garde" élites in urban centres. Its shock waves were disproportionate to its size. How can we explain the speed and extent of modernism's success?

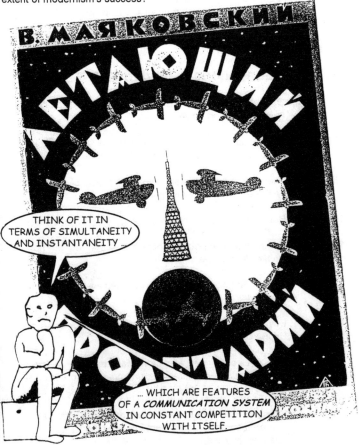

Of course, radical modernist changes in visual art, literature, music and architecture do not occur at exactly the same moment for each. But the coincidences are enough to persuade us of a *shared climate* of experimentation in all these sectors.

We are still left with three problems: (1) plural modern**isms**; (2) their **continuity**; (3) their decline and **end**. We need a time-scale. A rough and ready one is provided by Henri Lefèbvre.

"The absolute sovereignty of modernism is ushered in around 1910 by a rupture with the classical and traditional vocabulary [...] The reign is consolidated after World War I: cubism, abstract art, the rise of the Bauhaus, etc. ... That reign lasts until the 60s and 70s: then another reign is ushered in."

Cultural Foundations of Modernism

c. 1890: Opposing senses of *progress*, *crisis* and *transition* combine in the term "modernism".

1863: Anticipation of modernism in the art criticism of Charles Baudelaire, "The Painter of Modern Life".

1872: The term **Impressionism** coined for a style of art that will be the prototype of avant-gardism.

1879: Henrik Ibsen puts feminism on stage with *A Doll's House*.

1883: Friedrich Nietzsche announces the "superman" in *Thus Spake Zarathustra*.

1888: August Strindberg opposes Ibsen's feminism with his play *Miss Julie*.

1893: Edvard Munch's painting "The Cry" foreshadows Expressionism.

1894: Claude Debussy sets Stéphane Mallarmé's Symbolist poem *Prélude à l'après-midi d'un faune* to Impressionist music.

1900: Sigmund Freud inaugurates psychoanalysis with *The Interpretation of Dreams* (same year as the birth of quantum physics).

1901: Pablo Picasso in his pre-Cubist "Blue Period".

1902:	Alfred Stieglitz founds Photo-secession in New York and exhibits early modernist art from Europe.
1905:	**Les Fauves** ("Wild Beasts") group in Paris introduce an "expressionist" element in art ... In the same year, modernist **Expressionism** launches with **Die Brücke** ("The Bridge") group in Dresden, Germany.
1907:	Picasso's archetypal modernist artwork, "Les Demoiselles d'Avignon".
1908:	Picasso and Georges Braque begin work in **Cubism**.
1909:	Filippo Marinetti proclaims the first manifesto of **Futurism** in Paris.
1909–11:	Serge Diaghilev founds the modernist Ballets Russes that will tour Europe.
1910:	T.S. Eliot's poem "The Love Song of J. Alfred Prufrock" specifies the modernist element of cultural disenchantment.
1911:	Arnold Schoenberg's "Six Little Piano Pieces", Op. 19, pushes Expressionism in music to atonality and the beginnings of his 12-tone serial system.
1911:	Wassily Kandinsky and others found **Der Blaue Reiter** ("the Blue Rider") Expressionist art group in Munich (to which Schoenberg is allied).
1912:	Picasso produces his first collage work and Marcel Duchamp his "last painting", the mechanico-cubist "Nude Descending a Staircase".
1913:	Schoenberg's disciple Anton von Webern composes "Six Bagatelles for String Quartet", Op. 9, a three-and-a-half-minute work of atonal abstraction.
1913:	Kandinsky outlines the principles of abstraction in art, *On the Spiritual in Art*.

1913: Igor Stravinsky's music *The Rite of Spring* for Diaghilev's Ballets Russes causes a riot in Paris.

1913: The Armory Show – or International Exhibition of Modern Art – seen in New York, Chicago and Boston, introduces the American public and artists to the revolutionary avant-gardism of European art.

1914: James Joyce publishes his experimental short stories *Dubliners*.

1916: On the eve of the Russian Revolution, the anti-war and anarchic **Dadaism** founded in Zurich at the Cabaret Voltaire.

1917: Picasso works with poet Jean Cocteau, composer Erik Satie and Diaghilev's choreographer Léonide Massine on the ballet, "Parade".

1919: **United Artists** film studio founded in Hollywood by Charlie Chaplin, D.S. Griffiths, Mary Pickford and Douglas Fairbanks.

1920: **Groupe des Six** – composers including Arthur Honegger, Francis Poulenc, Darius Milhaud – return to music expressive of charm, wit and accessibility against the extremes of avant-gardism.

1921: Ludwig Wittgenstein publishes the key work of modernist logic that challenges all previous philosophy, *Tractatus Logico-Philosophicus*.

1921: Man Ray produces photographs without a camera, the Dadaist "Rayographs".

1922: The twin totems of modernist literature are published: James Joyce's *Ulysses* and T.S. Eliot's *The Waste Land*.

1924: André Breton issues his first *Surrealist Manifesto*.

1925: Sergei Eisenstein deploys the essence of modernist film techniques in *Battleship Potemkin*.

1925: The term **Neue Sachlichkeit** ("New Objectivity") coined to describe the extreme anguished realism of the post-war artists – George Grosz, Otto Dix and others in Germany.

1925–6: Modernism diversely manifested in American writings: F. Scott Fitzgerald's *The Great Gatsby*, John Dos Passos' *Manhattan Transfer*, Ernest Hemingway's *The Sun Also Rises*, and the experimental work of Gertrude Stein.

1926: Edgard Varese introduces a new "concrete" element into avant-garde music with *Arcana* and its effect on later "post-serial" composers like John Cage and Karlheinz Stockhausen.

1934: "The end" of modernism is decreed by Commissar Zhdanov in the Soviet Union.

1937: The Nazi exhibition of "degenerate art" ridicules and *criminalizes* modernism – is this another "end" of modernism?

1949: Senator George Dondero denounces modernism as a "Communist plot" to undermine America – the final "end" of modernism?

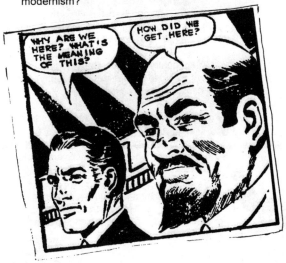

What is the Difference between Modernism and Modernity?

The first and simplest way to define modernity and distinguish it from modernism is in terms of new technologies – on a *mass* scale for *mass* consumption. Modernity in real terms means new modes of transport (the automobile, bus, aeroplane, tractor and underground train); new media (film, photography, the X-ray, telephone, typewriter, tape recorder); new materials (reinforced concrete, steel, plate glass, ready-mixed oil paint, plastic, dyes and man-made fibres); new sources of power and energy (oil and petroleum, electricity, the internal combustion engine, diesel engine and steam turbine).

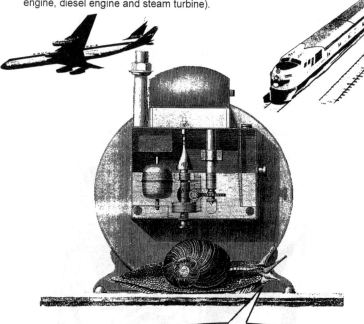

INCREASED SPEED SEEMS REFLECTED IN QUICKER CHANGES OF FASHION. IS THAT A COINCIDENCE?

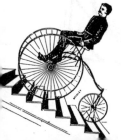

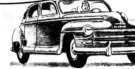

All these technologies give rise to a qualitatively different experience of "being modern". The 20th-century Western inhabitant speeds into totally new spheres – geographical, but also interpersonal, emotional and cultural.

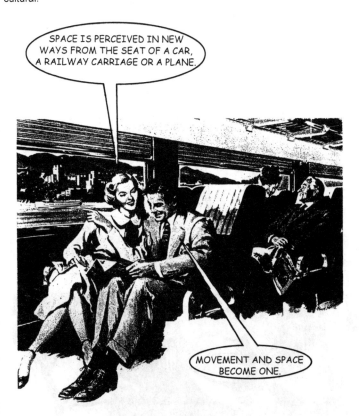

SPACE IS PERCEIVED IN NEW WAYS FROM THE SEAT OF A CAR, A RAILWAY CARRIAGE OR A PLANE.

MOVEMENT AND SPACE BECOME ONE.

Instead of cosy countryside or sweeping vistas, travellers and urban dwellers are confronted by a kaleidoscopic collage of sights and sounds. What was previously contained in separate spaces is now mixed up.

Technologies of Time

Perception of time in modernity is radically changed. New technologies of management such as "Taylorism" and "Fordism" altered the way people behaved as "labouring units".

Taylorism refers to the application of scientific principles to the workplace by the American **Frederick W. Taylor** (1856–1915), elaborated in *The Principles of Scientific Management* (1911).

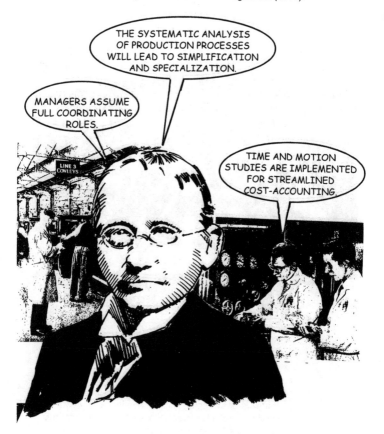

Fordism generally refers to the development of mass-production. It originated in the USA through the adoption of the assembly-line in the manufacture of cars by **Henry Ford** (1863–1947).

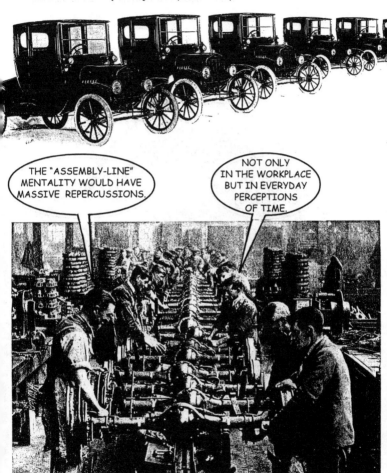

THE "ASSEMBLY-LINE" MENTALITY WOULD HAVE MASSIVE REPERCUSSIONS.

NOT ONLY IN THE WORKPLACE BUT IN EVERYDAY PERCEPTIONS OF TIME.

Standard Time

National time became known in 19th-century England as "Railway Time", as opposed to idiosyncratic localized time. Railways were run according to fixed timetables, but you could change "time zones" if you travelled from, say, London to Bristol.

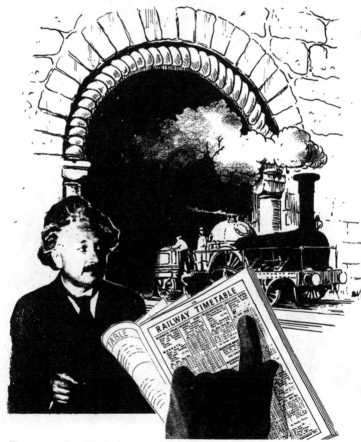

Time was rationalized when world-wide standards of time were fixed and agreed in the International Conference on Time in 1912.

The driving force behind all these developments in modern technology was the mega-capitalist entrepreneur: industrialists like **Henry Rockefeller** (1839–1937) and **John Pierpont Morgan** (1837–1913) in the USA; **William Lever/Lord Leverhulme** (1851–1925) in Britain; and the **Krupp** family in Germany.

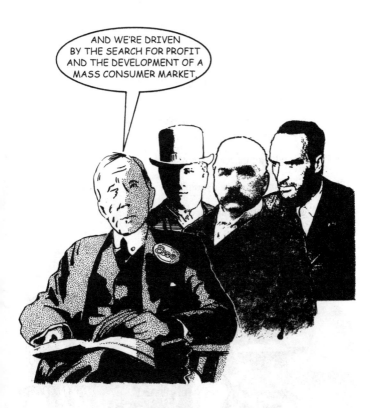

The streamlined factory floor, the artificially-lit office environment, clattering away to the sound of regimented typewriters, were geared to servicing the growing and insatiable needs of an urbanized and industrialized workforce.

Key Inventions of Modernity

1843: I.K. Brunel designs first propeller-driven steam ship to cross the Atlantic. Cunard steam-lines introduce regular passenger service after 1855.

1857: Louis Pasteur announces his germ theory of disease.

1858: Charles Nadar takes first aerial photograph from a balloon.

1858: Start of laying the trans-Atlantic telegraphic cable.

1864: Chromolithography printing for the colour reproduction of paintings in books.

1865: Gregor Mendel reports his findings on genetic inheritance factors – later called "alleles" of genes.

1865: Joseph Lister introduces anti-septic techniques in surgery.

1867: Alfred Nobel invents dynamite.

1869: Trans-continental railway in the USA.

1869: Opening of the Suez Canal.

1872: Bacteriology founded by Ferdinand Cohn.

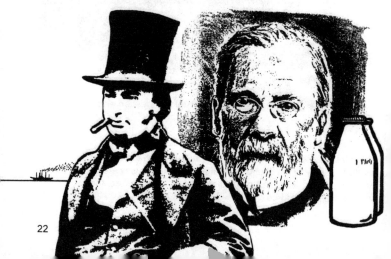

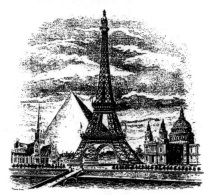

1873: James Clerk Maxwell unifies electromagnetism and light in one set of equations.

1874: Wilhelm Wundt founds experimental psychology.

1874: Remington & Sons produce first commercial typewriter which, together with stenography and other inventions, will revolutionize mass office work.

1876: Alexander Graham Bell invents telephone.

1877: Thomas Alva Edison invents phonograph.

1878: George Eastman invents dry photographic plates.

1879: Edison invents electric light bulb.

1882: Standard Oil trust formed.

1884: London Undergound railway opened.

1885: G.W. Daimler invents the internal combustion engine and in 1890 founds car manufacture company.

1888: George Eastman patents the Kodak box camera.

1889: Edison invents kinetoscope.

1889: Eiffel Tower completed for the Paris World Exposition.

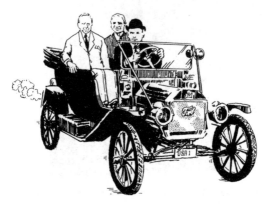

1890: First skyscraper using steel skeleton designed by Louis Sullivan in St Louis, USA.

1892: H.A. Lorentz announces the electron theory.

1894: Wilhelm Roentgen discovers x-rays.

1895: First public motion-picture film screening by Louis and Auguste Lumière, developed from Edison's inventions.

1895: Guglielmo Marconi invents wireless telegraphy.

1897: Joseph John Thomson discovers the electron by experiment.

1898: Marie and Pierre Curie discover radium.

1900: Max Planck initiates quantum theory in his study of electromagnetic radiation energy.

1901: Marconi transmits first trans-Atlantic radio wave signals.

1903: Orville and Wilbur Wright perform first successful aeroplane flight.

1903: Henry Ford opens Ford Motor Company and begins assembly-line production of the Model 'T' car in 1912.

1904: Ira Rubel invents offset lithography.

1905: Albert Einstein publishes his *Special Theory of Relativity* and in 1915 his *General Principles of Relativity* with its revolutionary model of non-Euclidean 4-dimensional space-time.

1909: Louis Blériot is the first to fly across the English Channel in a monoplane.

1913: Niels Bohr applies quantum theory to the structure of the atom.

1914: Opening of the Panama Canal.

1926: R.H. Goddard designs and flies first liquid-fuelled rocket.

1927: Charles Lindbergh performs first solo trans-Atlantic flight from New York to Paris in a monoplane.

1928: Alexander Fleming discovers penicillin.

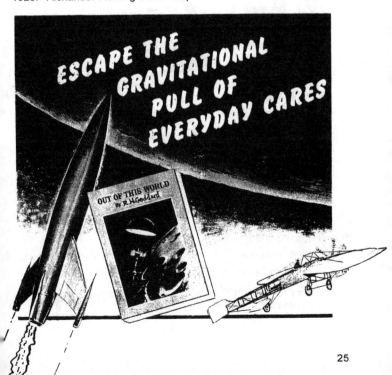

The New Industrial Art

Advertising, particularly in the USA, transformed itself from a mere commercial accessory to a key industry in its own right. And not just an industry, but a medium for constructing and representing a world of desires, aspirations and surrogate identities. Very quickly, these "hidden persuaders" of mass consumerist society exploited all the strategies of modernism to create a new pop medium: filmic techniques of montage, avant-garde design, manifesto one-liners, jazz tunes – but especially psychoanalysis.

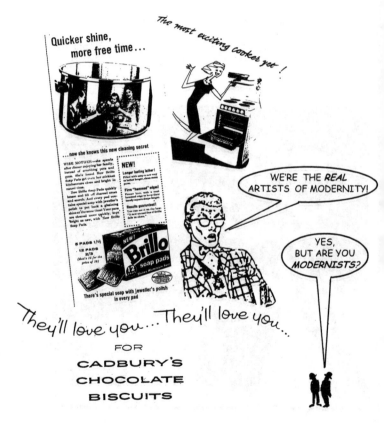

But is technology all there is to "modernity"? Can we see the Russian Revolution of 1917 as an experiment in modernity? What about the Nazi Holocaust in the 1940s? Was that modernity in its application of managerial Taylorism and assembly-line Fordism to the extermination of millions? Isn't the A-bomb quintessential modernity?

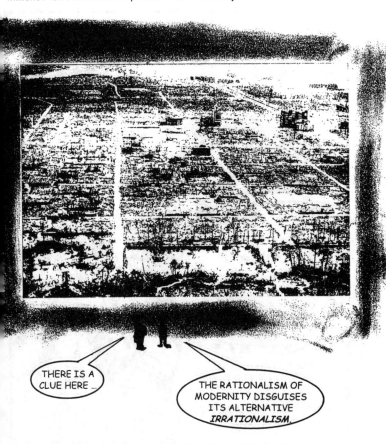

THERE IS A CLUE HERE ...

THE RATIONALISM OF MODERNITY DISGUISES ITS ALTERNATIVE *IRRATIONALISM*.

Living in modernity is perhaps enough to make one "modern" but not necessarily a "modernist". Modernism probes deeper into the unconscious layers of modernity and confronts it with its own hidden anxieties.

So … How does Modernism Fit into All This?

This is a key question – and not easy to answer. Modernism isn't simply a knee-jerk reaction to modernity. It doesn't simply reflect, but also sets itself against, modernity.

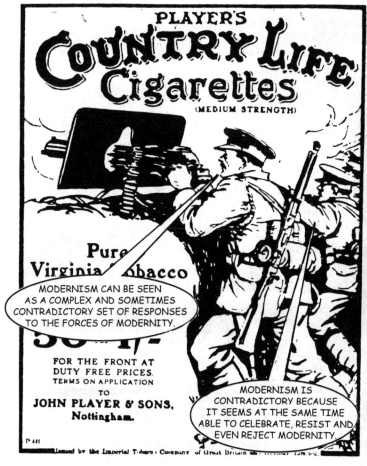

For the moment we shall look at some examples of how modernity was taken up in a *positive* manner.

What is striking about the great modernists is not just a confidence in their own abilities, in their "genius", but in the capacity of their work to be innovative and progressive.

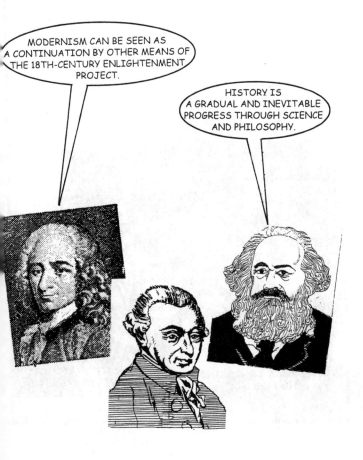

MODERNISM CAN BE SEEN AS A CONTINUATION BY OTHER MEANS OF THE 18TH-CENTURY ENLIGHTENMENT PROJECT.

HISTORY IS A GRADUAL AND INEVITABLE PROGRESS THROUGH SCIENCE AND PHILOSOPHY.

An Experimentalist Attitude

The avant-gardists were sure of the value of their exploratory work as being part of a progressive unveiling of the truth of the modern world. They possessed a supreme self-consciousness of being part of a new set of sensibilities, a new way of looking at the world. Many had an almost scientific attitude to research: not experiment for experiment's sake, but rather …

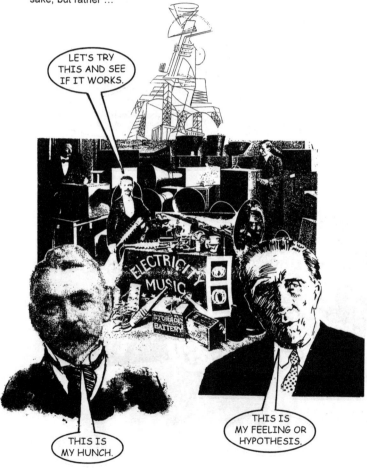

Italian **Futurism** was one of the earliest modernist movements which wholeheartedly embraced and aggressively celebrated the modern utopia made up of machines, revolution, movement and speed.

Futurism's rejection of "antiquated Europe" seems dedicated to an idealized vision of progress. But you don't have to dig deep or wait long for it to show its true colours – a lunatic "primitivism" that glories in total mechanized war, an élite of supermen and all the other symptoms of jackboot Fascism that it will enthusiastically endorse in the 1920s.

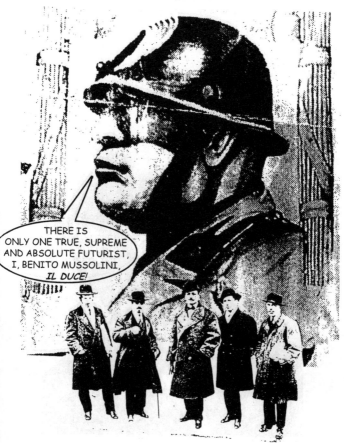

Simultaneous Futurism

F.T. Marinetti (1876–1944) was the inspired publicist, spokesman and poet for the Futurists. He published the "First Futurist Manifesto" in the Paris newspaper *Le Figaro* in 1909.

We will sing the great masses agitated by work, pleasure or revolt; we will sing the multicoloured and polyphonic surf of revolutions in modern capitals; the nocturnal vibration of docks and arsenals beneath their glaring electric moons; greedy stations devouring smoking serpents; factories hanging from the clouds by the threads of their smoke; bridges like giant gymnasts stepping over sunny rivers sparkling like diabolical cutlery; adventurous steamers scenting the horizon; large-breasted locomotives bridled with long tubes, and the slippery flight of airplanes whose propellers have flaglike flutterings and applauses of enthusiastic crowds.

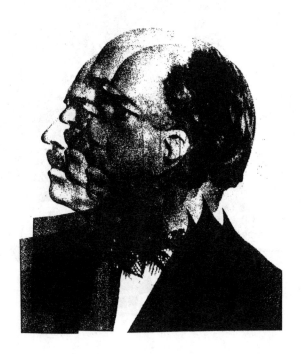

Italian Futurism, although a distinct movement, had wide ramifications. Its celebratory style is echoed in the manifesto of the **Rayonists** (a Russian movement of 1913) which intended to synthesize Cubism, Futurism and **Orphism** (1911–14).

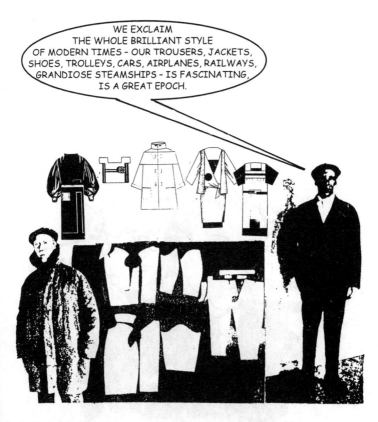

WE EXCLAIM THE WHOLE BRILLIANT STYLE OF MODERN TIMES – OUR TROUSERS, JACKETS, SHOES, TROLLEYS, CARS, AIRPLANES, RAILWAYS, GRANDIOSE STEAMSHIPS – IS FASCINATING, IS A GREAT EPOCH.

Again, there is a breathless evocation of things and machines, all existing in the simultaneous present. This idea of simultaneity is encountered again and again in modernist writing, painting, music and theatre. It is an expression of modernity in its over-abundance of images and sounds jostling for attention in the city.

Architecture: Functionalist Modernism

Architecture fully embodied the technological impetus of modernity by its use of such new building materials as reinforced concrete and plate glass, but also in its functional attitude to the modern environment with all its new forms of transport and communication, new urban social groupings, new relations to the workplace and home.

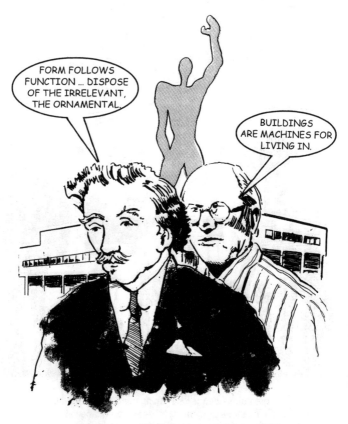

Adolf Loos (1870–1933), in his *Ornament and Crime* (1908), voiced the essence of architectural modernism: he equated decoration with criminality.

Le Corbusier, perhaps the best-known modernist architect, provides a forceful architectural manifesto in his Preface to *L'Urbanisme* (*The City of Tomorrow*, 1924). It tells how he goes for a stroll on an autumn evening in 1924 and finds that because of the traffic he cannot cross the Champs Elysées, a Paris boulevard. "I think back to my youth as a student: the road belonged to us then; we sang in it, we argued in it, while the horse-bus flowed softly by …" But this is not a lament.

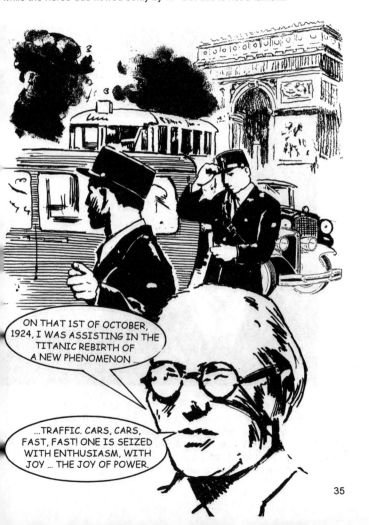

Giedion's Bible

This conjoining of machine travel and aesthetics is a constant reference point in the elaboration of different modernist art forms. Here is **Sigfried Giedion** (1888–1968), writing in 1939 about Robert Moses, a New York urban planner, in the book that became the bible of modern architecture, *Space, Time and Architecture*.

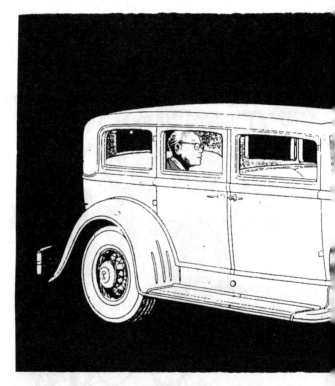

"As with many of the creations born out of the spirit of this age, the meaning and beauty of the parkway cannot be grasped from a single point of observation, as was possible from a window in the chateau of Versailles. It can be revealed only by movement, by going along in a steady flow, as the rules of traffic prescribe. The space-time feeling of our period can seldom be felt so keenly as when driving."

The exemplary modern phenomenon of cinema not only reproduces "moving pictures" of the world, but constructs new technologies of *seeing*.

One of the first publicly screened films, **Louis Lumière**'s (1864–1948) "A Train Entering the Station" (1895), gave rise to the legend that spectators rushed away from the screen in fright as the train bore down on them.

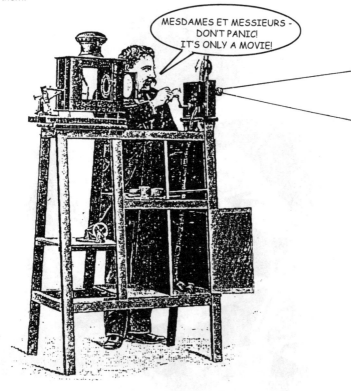

The coincidence of new transport technologies with new techniques of entertainment is visible in the fact that many of the very early films are train films, made by cameras fixed to the locomotive rushing through the landscape.

Sticking Things Together

The technique of collage is another example of the way in which modern life seeps into modernist works. Picasso and **Georges Braque** (1882–1963) physically incorporated pieces of the outside world, torn newspaper headlines and other urban debris within their paintings.

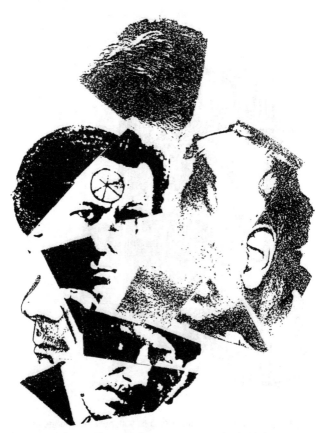

Kurt Schwitters (1887–1948) devoted his whole life to collecting and collaging the detritus of everyday life, which he called *Merz*, itself from a torn bit of paper that read "Com*merz*".

Such a "collage" tactic is comparable to the way in which writers such as **Guillaume Apollinaire** (1880–1918) or T.S. Eliot worked. They allowed overheard snatches of dialogue to enter the space of a poem, and re-worked slang and argotic expressions of everyday encounters into the texture of their prose and verse.

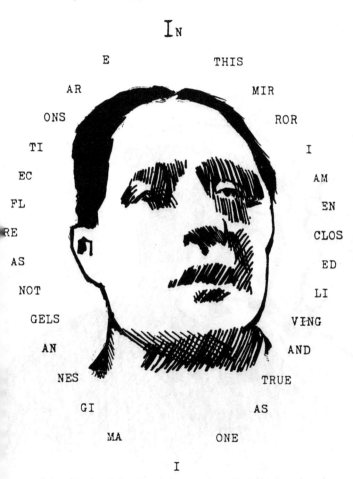

Tatlin's Tower

In Soviet Russia, the artist **Vladimir Tatlin** (1885–1953) engineered a work which expressed the modern vision of socialism. His tower, entitled *Monument to the Third International*, was designed in 1919. Although never built, it has remained an icon of a heroic modernism which attempted to fuse revolutionary ideology, technology and aesthetics.

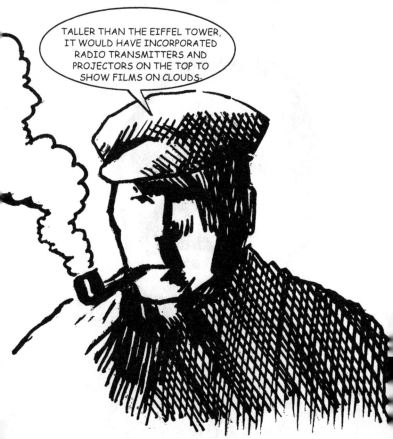

TALLER THAN THE EIFFEL TOWER, IT WOULD HAVE INCORPORATED RADIO TRANSMITTERS AND PROJECTORS ON THE TOP TO SHOW FILMS ON CLOUDS.

It was a positive statement about the future. The spiral which ran around the tower expressed "the modern spirit of the age".

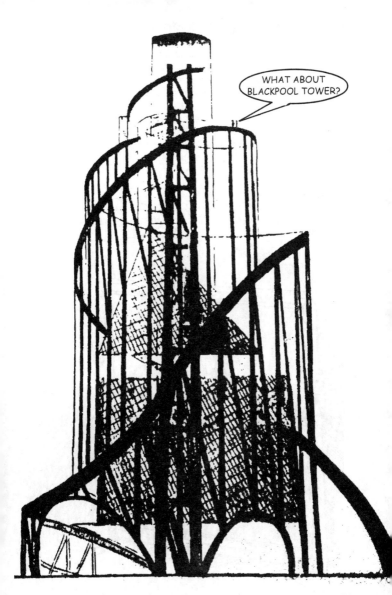

41

How do we Recognize a Modernist Work?

This is another key question. Let's start with Picasso's iconic work, "Les Demoiselles d'Avignon" (1907), which is "recognized" as the pioneering masterpiece of modernism in its heroic first phase before the First World War. The question is *why* is it recognized as specially modernist?

It was bigger than any of Picasso's previous paintings. It possessed a quality that we associate with that fundamental tool of modernism – the **manifesto**. It proclaimed itself, it exuded a confidence in its newness and radicality.

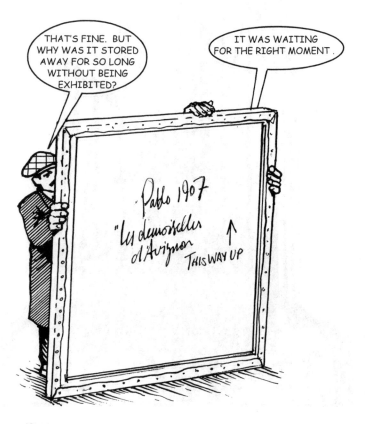

André Salmon, an art critic writing in 1912:

This painting has never been revealed to the public. It is composed of six large female nudes delineated with a severe accent. For the first time with Picasso the expression of the faces is neither tragic nor impassioned. They are masks almost completely devoid of humanity. However, these personages are not gods, neither are they Titans or heroes; they are not even allegorical or symbolical figures....

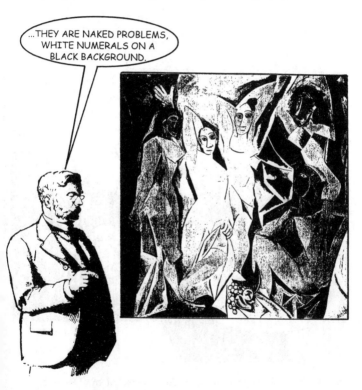

Salmon's last sentence sums up the move to **abstraction** which was to be a dominant feature of modernist painting. The figures are not allegorical or symbolic – their meaning must be read off the canvas, the *surface* of the picture.

The End of the Past

Always present is the idea of the "first time", the "new", and getting away from the past – even though the work itself might contain very strong traces of the old, the classical or the primitive. The Surrealist **André Breton** (1896–1966) said of Picasso's painting in 1920 …

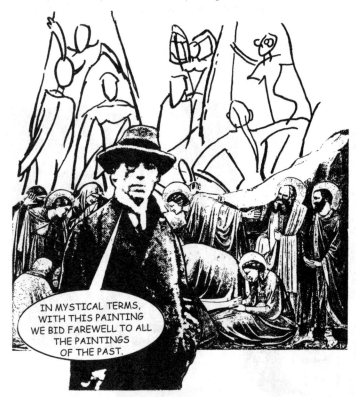

IN MYSTICAL TERMS, WITH THIS PAINTING WE BID FAREWELL TO ALL THE PAINTINGS OF THE PAST.

John Richardson, who has written the definitive biography of Picasso, put it like this: "… the most innovative painting since Giotto … it established a new pictorial syntax; it enabled people to perceive things with new eyes, new minds, new awareness. 'Les Demoiselles d'Avignon' is the first unequivocally 20th century masterpiece, a principal detonator of the modern movement, the cornerstone of 20th century art."

The pioneer modernist poet Guillaume Apollinaire, a contemporary and friend of Picasso's, wrote that "Picasso studies an object the way a surgeon dissects a corpse".

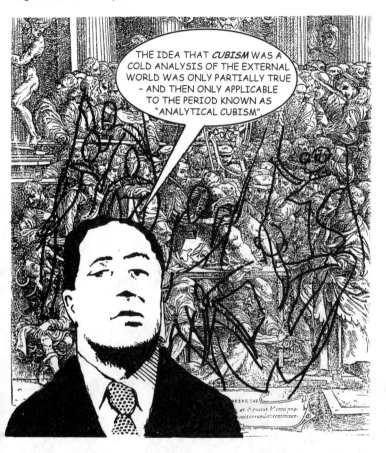

But what many artists (including Apollinaire) shared with Picasso and Braque was a concern with the "materiality" of art. "… a refusal to make of the work a transparent window on the world … paint, lines, words assume a new kind of self-sufficiency and we are not invited to look beyond the work for something to explain or legitimate."

Reading Picasso ...

"Les Demoiselles" is not really self-sufficient at all. Like all other modernist works, its meanings are only revealed to us as we bring other forms of reading and interpretations and references to bear on it. You can proceed to "read" the painting in sophisticated and meaningful ways, depending on your familiarity with art historical and cultural contexts and discourses.

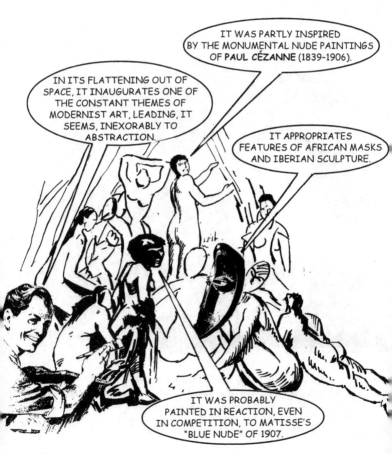

... and Reading Similarities

Can we identify similarities with other key modernist texts? Yes. In a similar way, two other works of the modernist movement were seen from the start – and continued to be so regarded – as iconic. T.S. Eliot's *The Waste Land* (1922) and James Joyce's *Ulysses* (1922) were ushered into the literary world through a premeditated and sophisticated networking of small magazines, booksellers and investors.

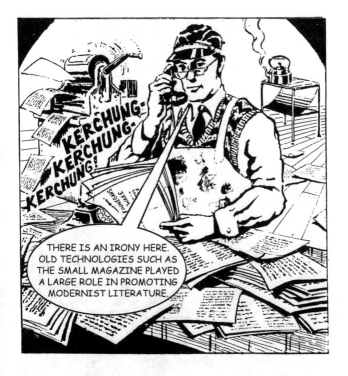

And a larger irony. These works, which originally signified cultural disruption and radically new ways of interpreting the world, are now recognized as part of the canon – an established tradition – of world literature. They have now become the "classic" set texts of university English Literature departments.

The Pleasure of the Text?

Common strands in these modernist works can be detected by focusing on how we try to *understand* them. They are all difficult. Compared to a 19th-century novel or painting, we have to work on the texts to discover what they are about.

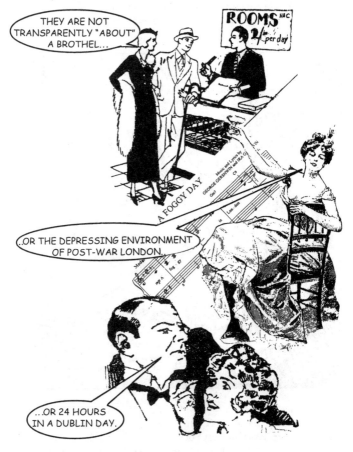

But neither are they just about formal or self-contained meanings – they *do* refer to a "thickness" of experience.

All three works make special demands on the viewer or reader. You need to work on the material – the words, the shapes – in order to gain the beginnings of an understanding.

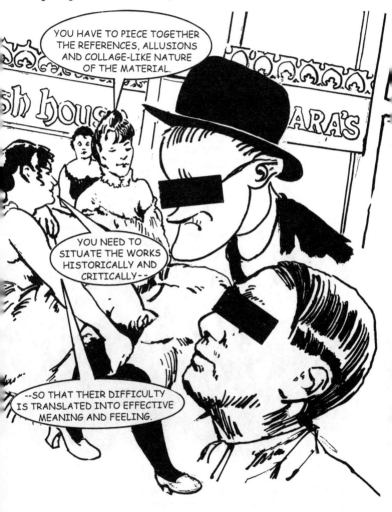

YOU HAVE TO PIECE TOGETHER THE REFERENCES, ALLUSIONS AND COLLAGE-LIKE NATURE OF THE MATERIAL.

YOU NEED TO SITUATE THE WORKS HISTORICALLY AND CRITICALLY--

--SO THAT THEIR DIFFICULTY IS TRANSLATED INTO EFFECTIVE MEANING AND FEELING.

How do the Arts Relate to Each Other?

There is a long history to the ways in which different art forms interrelate and compare with each other. The ancient Latin dictum, *ut pictura poesis* ("as in painting so in poetry"), had for centuries informed a cross-fertilization of artistic practices. The phrase, "all art aspires to the condition of music", was a 19th-century Romantic coinage. **Charles Baudelaire** (1821–67), a proto-modernist poet, experimented with *synaesthesia*, which means translating one sense perception into another.

... THE *COLOURS* OF MUSICAL TONES, THE *SOUND* OF PICTORIAL COLOUR TONES, THEIR SUGGESTIONS OF *SMELLS* AND *TASTES* ...

The ambition of *Gesamtkunstwerk* (a "total work of art") in the titanic operas of **Richard Wagner** (1813–83) gave impetus to the modernist fusion of the arts.

The cross-fertilization of modernist art forms was often expressed in tactical programmings of the **manifesto**. Such manifestos were delivered in vehemently multi-art form, as if to declare the universal applicability of a new aesthetic programme. Following the **Dadaists**, the **Futurists** in their promotional events were particularly adept at creating audio-visual cacophonies of meaning. They cleverly engineered "spontaneous" events. These boisterous and provocative "performance happenings" were in effect avant-garde music-hall self-promotions.

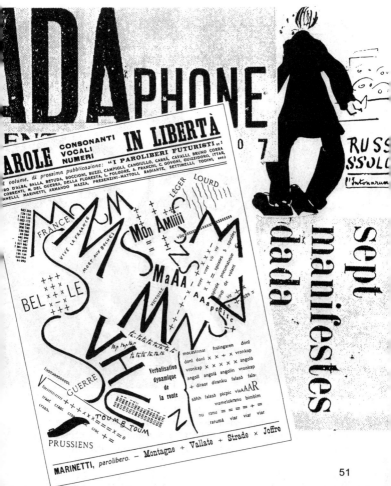

Multi-Artform Performances

Many of the most striking multi-artform collaborations were politically inspired. The Berlin productions of the theatre director **Erwin Piscator** (1893–1966), in his collaborations with the Marxist playwright **Bertolt Brecht** (1898–1956) and others, brought the arts into revolutionary convergence. A live collage took place between actors, music, decor and film.

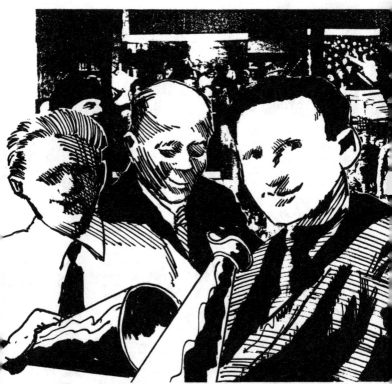

In the work of **El Lissitsky** (1890–1941), propaganda, photographs and slogans were combined in revolutionary word-picture posters and installations. T.J. Clark, one of the foremost art historians of modernism, calls Lissitsky's design for the Soviet Pavilion at the International Press Exhibition in Cologne in 1928 "the greatest of all Gesamtkunstwerks …"

Public art events were pretexts for the creative collaboration between artists from different domains. Such is the now legendary production of the ballet "Parade" of 1917. It involved – with a great deal of intrigue and back-biting – the combined and starry talents of **Jean Cocteau** (1889–1963) …

Pablo Picasso …

Erik Satie (1866–1925) …

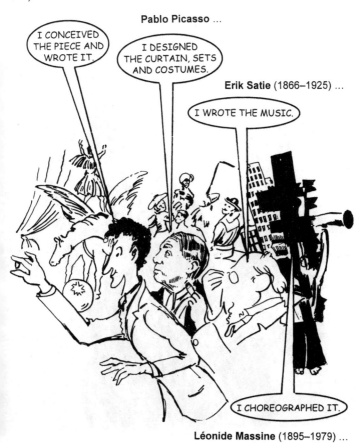

Léonide Massine (1895–1979) …

And **Serge Diaghilev**'s (1872–1929) Ballets Russes, who actually danced it.

A Spirit of Modernist Cooperation

There were countless other smaller-scale collaborations. For example, **Blaise Cendrars'** (1887–1961) use of artists such as **Sonia Delaunay** (1885–1979), **Francis Picabia** (1879–1953) and **Fernand Léger** (1881–1955) to provide complementary visualizations of his poems. Later on, he provided poems to accompany the photographs of **Robert Doisneau** (1912–94) in *The Suburbs of Paris* (1949).

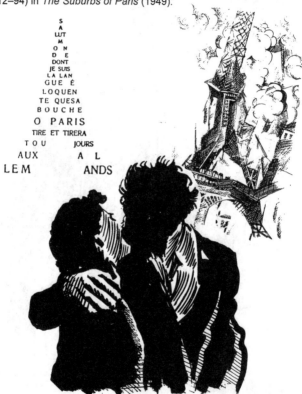

Often the mix between art forms took a playful turn. This was particularly striking in the attempts of typographically arranged poetry to mimic pictures. Apollinaire's inventive picture-poems sent from the war front were to inspire a minor modernist school of "concrete poetry".

Avant-garde Film-making

Film is a collaborative art-form in its very essence. The most famous example of avant-garde cooperation is the teaming together of Surrealist painter Salvador Dalí and film director **Luis Buñuel** (1900–83) to create the notorious *Un Chien Andalou* (1928) and *L'Âge d'Or* (1930).

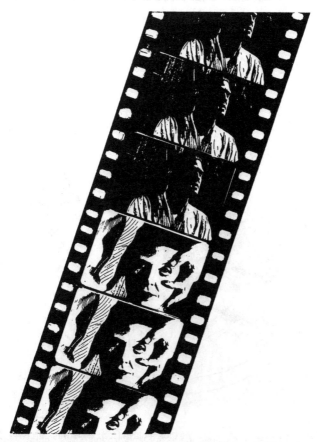

Abstract animation film-makers such as **Oskar Fischinger** (1900–67), **Len Lye** (1901–80) and **Norman McLaren** (1914–87) translated music into moving image sequences.

Towards Atonality and Abstraction

The synaesthetic link between music and painting had already been established by the Romantics. Modernism took the idea much further. Sound and colour were now seen as mutually informed by the same "tonal freedom" which explained the progress of both to *abstraction*.

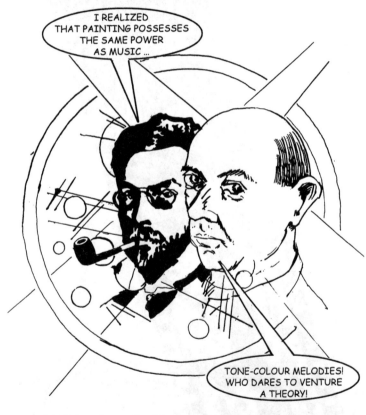

Arnold Schoenberg coined the term *Klangfarbenmelodie* (tone-colour melody) in 1911 as he broke with the conventional musical syntax of tonality, at the same time that **Wassily Kandinsky** (1866–1944) created his first abstract "compositions" in painting.

Schoenberg was associated with *Der Blaue Reiter* (the Blue Rider) school of Expressionism in Munich, founded c. 1911 by Kandinsky, **Franz Marc** (1880–1916), **Paul Klee** (1879–1940) and other artists. Marc at once grasped the correspondence between Schoenberg's atonal experiment and Kandinsky's abstraction.

"Can you imagine a music in which tonality (that is, the adherence to any key) is completely suspended? I was constantly reminded of Kandinsky's large *Composition*, which also permits no trace of tonality ... and also of Kandinsky's 'jumping spots' in hearing this music, which allows each tone sounded to stand on its own (a kind of *white canvas* between the spots of colour!). Schoenberg proceeds from the principle that the concepts of consonance and dissonance do not exist at all."

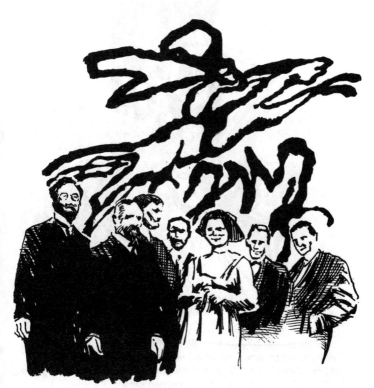

Is There a Modernist Theory in Relation to Practice?

We can see how modernist arts explain and sustain each other. But is there a deeper sense in which they stem from a common philosophy? Is there a unifying strand that can be said to be consistent throughout the arts?

The idea that art is "constructed" – that images and words do not represent the world transparently (as if from a window) – is a recurring theme. Cubist and Futurist artists focussed on the processes of vision in a changed modern environment.

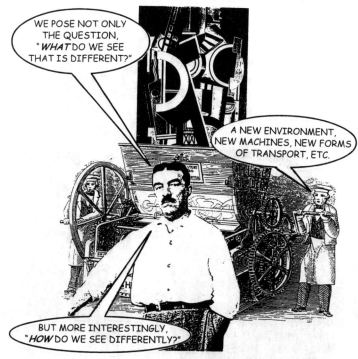

Artists did not provide a single answer to this question; but they all suggested by different pictorial strategies that the visual meaning of the world is not given, but built up and **constructed**.

A similar set of questions prompted the work of composers like Schoenberg, and avant-garde architects. But it is particularly explicit in the attitude of writers to language, in the work of novelists such as **James Joyce** (1882–1941) and **Gertrude Stein** (1874–1946), poets such as Blaise Cendrars and Ezra Pound, and the "words in freedom" project of the Futurists.

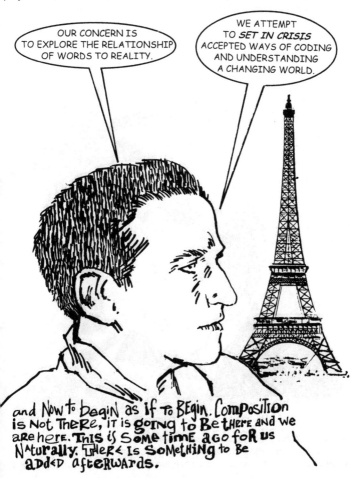

Structural Linguistics

The imaginative work of avant-garde modernists can be seen to connect with the *structural linguistics* of **Ferdinand de Saussure** (1857–1913). In his *Cours de Linguistique Générale*, published in 1916, he analysed how language is constructed in its relation to reality. His most basic idea concerns the relationship between the **signifier** and **signified**.

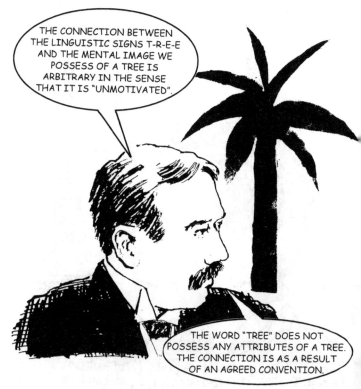

THE CONNECTION BETWEEN THE LINGUISTIC SIGNS T-R-E-E AND THE MENTAL IMAGE WE POSSESS OF A TREE IS ARBITRARY IN THE SENSE THAT IT IS "UNMOTIVATED".

THE WORD "TREE" DOES NOT POSSESS ANY ATTRIBUTES OF A TREE. THE CONNECTION IS AS A RESULT OF AN AGREED CONVENTION.

Another Saussurean principle is that meaning in language only arises from differences and relationships along the chain of signifiers. Modernists who subverted the conventions of language were agreeing with Saussure's view of its "arbitrary constructedness".

There isn't a simple causal fit between Saussurean linguistics and the creative play with words of so many modernist writers. The irony is that no modernists knew of Saussure, who only became important posthumously with the development of structuralism, semiology and post-structuralism.

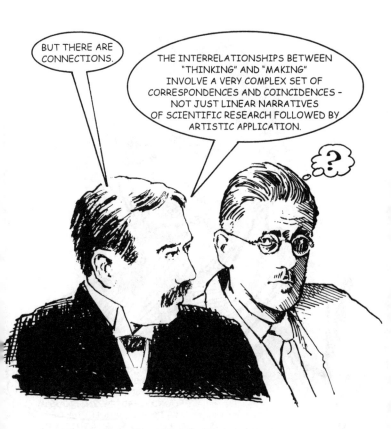

Another influential linguist from a succeeding generation, **Roman Jakobson** (1896–1982), was to combine in his writings an interest in the science of linguistics and in the semantic dislocations of modernist poets.

The Relation of Modernism to Philosophy

The complex interplay between theory and creative practice is also apparent in the connections between modernist practitioners and the work of key modern philosophers. Sometimes the coincidence of aims is implicit. This is Brecht on Marx …

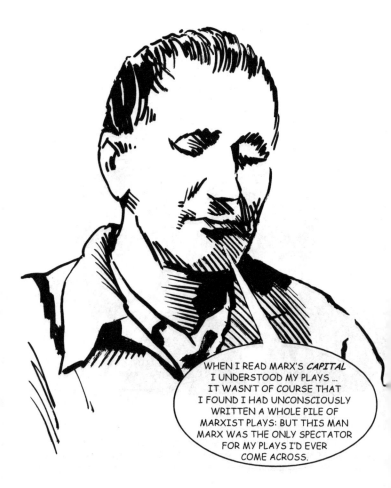

WHEN I READ MARX'S *CAPITAL* I UNDERSTOOD MY PLAYS … IT WASN'T OF COURSE THAT I FOUND I HAD UNCONSCIOUSLY WRITTEN A WHOLE PILE OF MARXIST PLAYS: BUT THIS MAN MARX WAS THE ONLY SPECTATOR FOR MY PLAYS I'D EVER COME ACROSS.

Philosophers such as **Ludwig Wittgenstein** (1889–1951), **Henri Bergson** (1859–1941), **Edmund Husserl** (1859–1938), **Martin Heidegger** (1889–1976) and others exerted all kinds of influence – some profound, others superficial – on modernist intellectuals and artists.

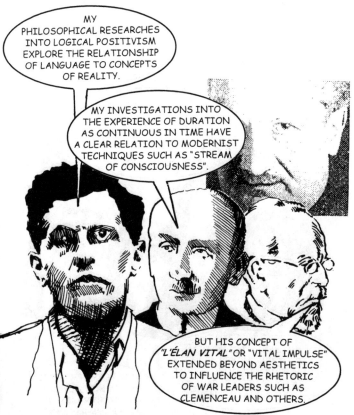

MY PHILOSOPHICAL RESEARCHES INTO LOGICAL POSITIVISM EXPLORE THE RELATIONSHIP OF LANGUAGE TO CONCEPTS OF REALITY.

MY INVESTIGATIONS INTO THE EXPERIENCE OF DURATION AS CONTINUOUS IN TIME HAVE A CLEAR RELATION TO MODERNIST TECHNIQUES SUCH AS "STREAM OF CONSCIOUSNESS".

BUT HIS CONCEPT OF *"L'ÉLAN VITAL"* OR "VITAL IMPULSE" EXTENDED BEYOND AESTHETICS TO INFLUENCE THE RHETORIC OF WAR LEADERS SUCH AS CLEMENCEAU AND OTHERS.

Husserl was the first to develop **phenomenology**: fundamentally, it differs from **rationalism** and **idealism** in concentrating on the perception of things in themselves. Heidegger, now more renowned for his dubious involvement with the Nazi party, extended the work of his teacher, Husserl, into dense and sometimes notoriously obscure explorations of the "question of being".

63

Science and Sociology

Not only philosophers contributed to the modernist structure of feeling. There is an enormous range of 20th-century scientists, sociologists and other thinkers. Among the key figures is **Albert Einstein** (1879–1955).

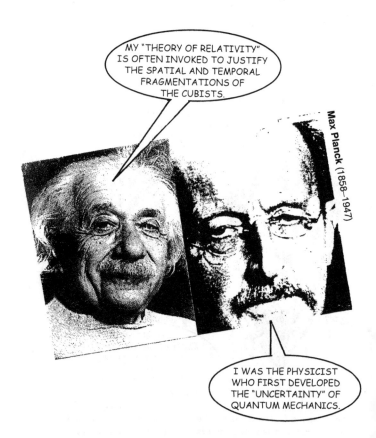

MY "THEORY OF RELATIVITY" IS OFTEN INVOKED TO JUSTIFY THE SPATIAL AND TEMPORAL FRAGMENTATIONS OF THE CUBISTS.

Max Planck (1858–1947)

I WAS THE PHYSICIST WHO FIRST DEVELOPED THE "UNCERTAINTY" OF QUANTUM MECHANICS.

Emile Durkheim (1858–1917) and **Max Weber** (1864–1920) were two founding fathers of sociology. **Antonio Gramsci** (1891–1937), whose intelligence Mussolini wanted to lock up for twenty years, provided original re-workings of Marxist thinking on politics and culture.

What About Marx, Nietzsche and ...?

Marshall Berman's stimulating book on modernism, *All That Is Solid Melts Into Air* (1982), controversially suggested that the key progenitors and players of modernism were located in the 19th century. Berman argued that Goethe, Marx, Nietzsche, Baudelaire and Dostoevsky were open to the contradictions of modern society. Although they attack this environment ...

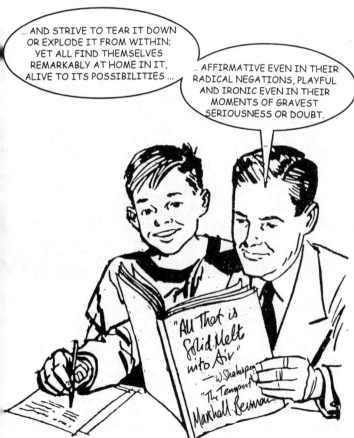

... AND STRIVE TO TEAR IT DOWN OR EXPLODE IT FROM WITHIN; YET ALL FIND THEMSELVES REMARKABLY AT HOME IN IT, ALIVE TO ITS POSSIBILITIES ...

.. AFFIRMATIVE EVEN IN THEIR RADICAL NEGATIONS, PLAYFUL AND IRONIC EVEN IN THEIR MOMENTS OF GRAVEST SERIOUSNESS OR DOUBT.

Cross-Currents of Influences

All of these key thinkers can be seen to influence a diverse range of imaginative and intellectual activity. But the form and nature of those influences are complex and not always easy to map. Sometimes the area of influence is delimited geographically.

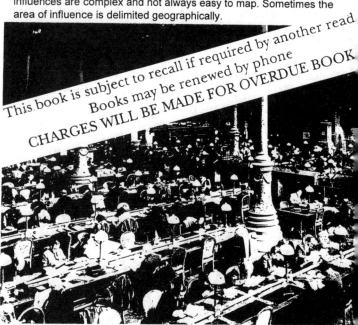

The German philosopher **G.W.F. Hegel** (1770–1831) heavily influenced the direction of philosophy not only in Germany, but, through the teachings of **Alexandre Kojève** (1902–68), for a whole generation of modern philosophers in France as well. Similarly, the phenomenological tradition stemming from Husserl and his disciple Martin Heidegger had an immense influence on continental philosophers and writers – including **Maurice Merleau-Ponty** (1907–61) and **Jean-Paul Sartre** (1905–80) – but was largely ignored in England. Bergson, with his concept of *l'élan vital*, had a preponderant influence in France. Wittgenstein and the whole tradition of Viennese logical positivism, which concentrated on the interrelationships between language, logic and reality, made its mark primarily in the English-speaking world.

Literary Cross-overs

There are many examples of modernist writers, novelists and poets who engaged in criticism and theory. **Henry James** (1843–1916), in the prefaces to his late books, expresses the modernist sensibility as it operates in the novel. **Virginia Woolf**'s (1882–1941) essays, "Mr. Bennett and Mrs. Brown" and "Modern Fiction", provide insights into how the modernist spirit interacts with the modern world. T.S. Eliot's essays complement his poetry. The French writer **Raymond Queneau** (1903–76) and the Mexican writer **Octavio Paz** (1914–98) switch from theory to poetry at a stroke of the pen. The work of the Argentinian **Jorge Luis Borges** (1899–1986) can be seen as the translation of modernist philosophy into short story form.

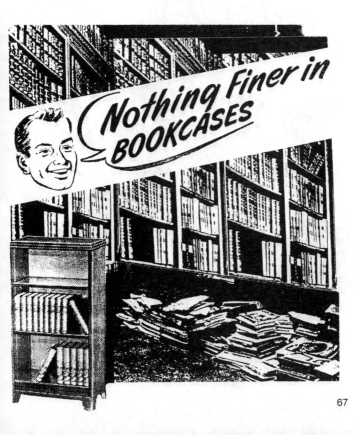

The synergy between theory and imagination works both ways. For example, the writings of the great French anthropologist **Claude Lévi-Strauss** (b. 1908) function on more than just the academic register. *Tristes Tropiques* (*The World on the Wane*, 1955) is as much an autobiographical voyage as it is a philosophical and anthropological exploration. Octavio Paz commented on reading Lévi-Strauss's book, *Le Cru et le cuit* (*The Raw and the Cooked*, 1964) …

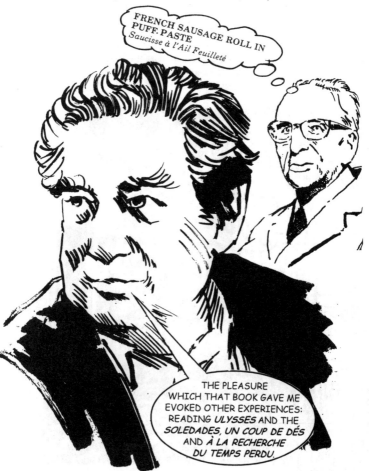

What is the Relation of Modernism to Primitivism?

There is another link to theory – not to carefully articulated philosophies, but a "deep" link to feelings and ideas. These are contained in the cluster of concepts around "primitivism" and the irrational.

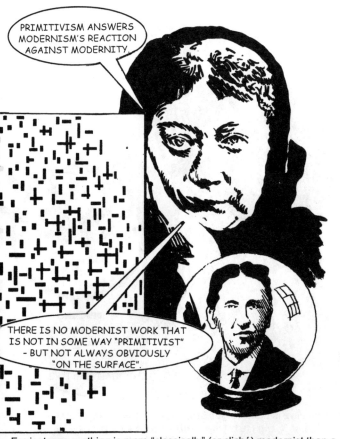

PRIMITIVISM ANSWERS MODERNISM'S REACTION AGAINST MODERNITY.

THERE IS NO MODERNIST WORK THAT IS NOT IN SOME WAY "PRIMITIVIST" – BUT NOT ALWAYS OBVIOUSLY "ON THE SURFACE".

For instance, nothing is more "classically" (or cliché) modernist than a **Piet Mondrian** (1872–1944) painting, and yet it springs from Theosophical occultism, a sort of deviant primitivism.

Is Primitivism Ethnocentric?

Primitivism can be seen as **ethnocentric** – judging all things, including people and their values, from your own socially and culturally defined standpoint – and implicated in **colonialist discourses** which signify, among other things, preoccupations and anxieties about sexuality and the instincts.

You can see the "primitive" in its most obvious form in Picasso's 1907 painting, "Les Demoiselles d'Avignon".

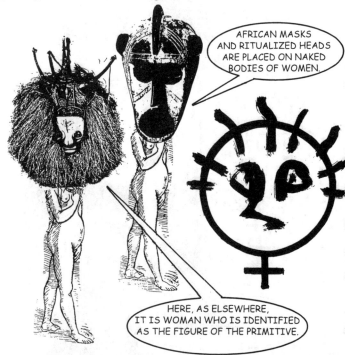

AFRICAN MASKS AND RITUALIZED HEADS ARE PLACED ON NAKED BODIES OF WOMEN.

HERE, AS ELSEWHERE, IT IS WOMAN WHO IS IDENTIFIED AS THE FIGURE OF THE PRIMITIVE.

The primitive is there in **Igor Stravinsky**'s (1882–1971) ballet music, *The Rite of Spring* (1912). It's there in bogus form (as Eliot himself admitted in the 1950s) in the references to **James Frazer**'s (1854–1941) book on primitive myths (*The Golden Bough*) in Eliot's notes to *The Waste Land*.

The group of artists known as the *Fauves* (French for "wild beasts") – in particular **Henri Matisse** (1869–1954), **André Derain** (1880–1954) and **Maurice de Vlaminck** (1876–1958) – are credited with being the first artists who systematically incorporated African art into their work.

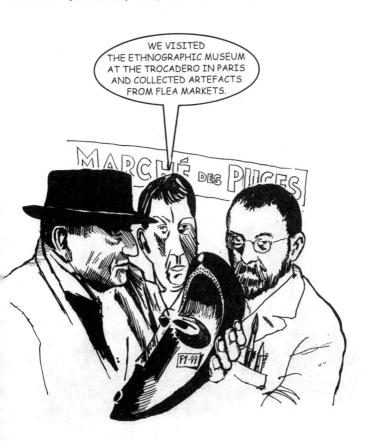

This other "naïve" popular art was, for them, both a return to the innocence of things child-like and a release into the primal and edenic "*luxe, calme et volupté*" (a title of one of Matisse's paintings).

Expressionist Primitivism

"**The Bridge**" (*Die Brücke*), an Expressionist school of painters formed in Dresden in 1905, was heavily influenced by African and Oceanic art – as well as by the paintings of **Vincent van Gogh** (1853–90) and **Paul Gauguin** (1848–1903). This work was available to view in the Dresden Ethnographic Museum. **Ernst Kirchner** (1880–1938) and **Erich Heckel** (1883–1970) were its best-known members.

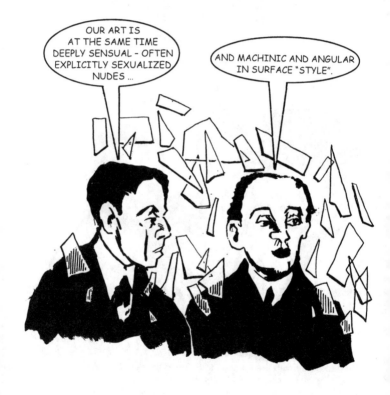

You can see this tension or contradiction in Heckel's *Day of Glass* (1913), which depicts a nude woman (a cypher for woman as nature and as the "noble savage"), immersed in a landscape of glass-like shards.

The conflation of the primitive with masculinist sexuality, colonialism and the physical act of creating a painting is extraordinarily present in Kandinsky's account of learning to paint.

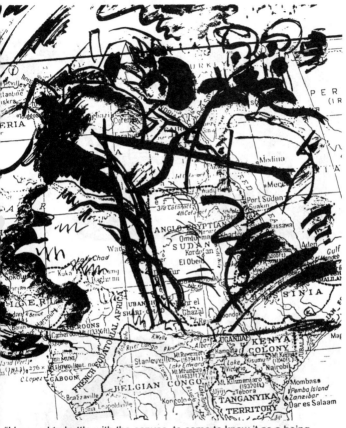

"I learned to battle with the canvas, to come to know it as a being resisting my wish (= dream), and to bend it forcibly to this wish. At first it stands there like a pure chaste virgin with clear eye and heavenly joy … And then comes the wilful brush which first here, then there, gradually conquers it with all the energy peculiar to it, like a European colonist, who pushes into the wild virgin nature, hitherto untouched, using axe, spade, hammer, and saw to shape it to his wishes."

Primitivism in Literature

The primitive can be suggested in more oblique and knowing ways, as on the title page of Eliot's 1925 poem, "The Hollow Men", which quotes the opening of **Joseph Conrad**'s (1857–1924) novella, "Heart of Darkness" (1899).

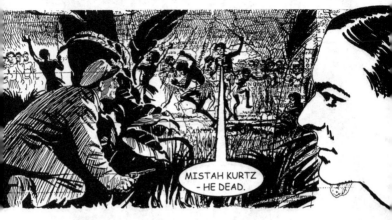

Or we can look to the novels of D.H. Lawrence, which celebrate the primitive as the atavistic and the authentic.

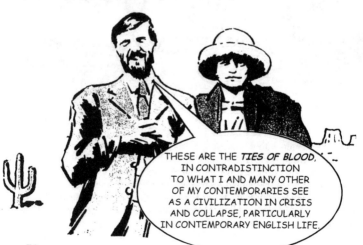

The representation and evocation of the "primitive" is full of contradictions. In the landscape paintings of **Emil Nolde** (1867–1956), Expressionist primitivism exerts its presence through intense, flowing colour. But the darker side of modernist politics insinuates itself in a revealing manner.

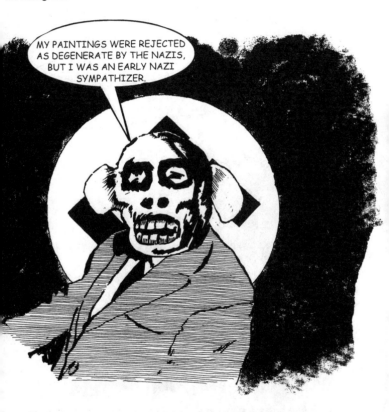

One could trace a connection between his anti-cerebral Expressionist paintings and the Fascistic appeal to the emotions and deep tribal roots. Similarly, one could consider **Leni Riefensthal**'s (b. 1902) cinematographic hymn to Hitler, *Triumph of the Will* (1933) and her post-war photographic celebration of African Nubian warriors to be of one piece.

What is the Relation of Modernism to Psychoanalysis?

Max Nordau (1849–1923) provided an authoritative psychiatric diagnosis of *fin-de-siècle* modernism in his vast work *Entartung* (*Degeneration*, 1892). He condemns the entire European élite in art, music and literature to incurable degeneracy, organic debility and cretinism.

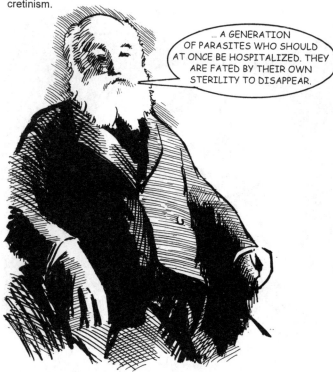

... A GENERATION OF PARASITES WHO SHOULD AT ONCE BE HOSPITALIZED. THEY ARE FATED BY THEIR OWN STERILITY TO DISAPPEAR.

The modern arts are symptoms of degenerate "atavisms" that in the future will be of no interest to a rationally progressive (i.e. "healthy") world. A crucially negative view of modernism existed from the start – not as an energy vitalized by modernity but an *unfitness from decadent exhaustion*. Psychiatry, in alliance with Social Darwinist theories in criminology and eugenics, proclaimed grave anxieties about Europe's racial "state of health".

The Primitivism of Sigmund Freud

Sigmund Freud (1856–1939) introduced a modernist psycho-dynamic alternative to late 19th-century psychiatry's bio-determinist doom and gloom.

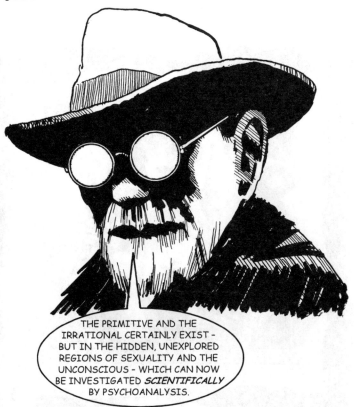

THE PRIMITIVE AND THE IRRATIONAL CERTAINLY EXIST – BUT IN THE HIDDEN, UNEXPLORED REGIONS OF SEXUALITY AND THE UNCONSCIOUS – WHICH CAN NOW BE INVESTIGATED *SCIENTIFICALLY* BY PSYCHOANALYSIS.

Freud's scientific quest was for a rational explanation and a humane "treatment" of what is so often apparently irrational in human behaviour. To do so, he adopted the modernist strategy of primitivism – for instance, using the myth of Oedipus to analyse narratives of childhood sexuality, or "dream interpretation" which harks back to ancient magical divination.

Freud's Influence

Freud's revolutionary views indelibly marked the century of modernism and modernity. His writings had an incalculable influence on the development of psychoanalysis as a therapy and as a scientific system of inquiry into human behaviour and cognition.

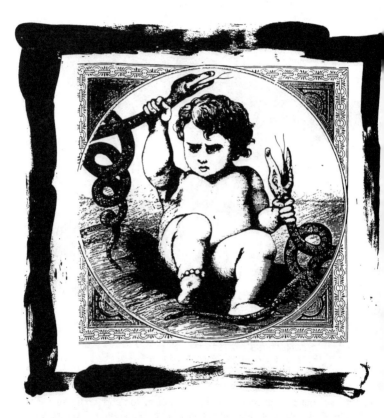

His ideas – we might almost say, his *invention* – of the unconscious (first conveyed in *The Interpretation of Dreams*, 1900), infantile sexuality, the Oedipus complex, fetishism and so much else were to provide a vast resource for succeeding generations of artists and thinkers.

What is the interest of Freud for writers as diverse as **Thomas Mann** (1875–1955), **Franz Kafka** (1883–1924) and **Georges Bataille** (1897–1962), or dramatists as opposed as **August Strindberg** (1849–1912) and **Alfred Jarry** (1873–1907), or painters as various as **Edvard Munch** (1863–1944), **Max Beckman** (1884–1950), **Otto Dix** (1891–1969), **Hans Bellmer** (1900–75), **Joan Miró** (1893–1983), **Salvador Dalí** (1904–89), **Giorgio de Chirico** (1888–1978) and **René Magritte** (1898–1967)?

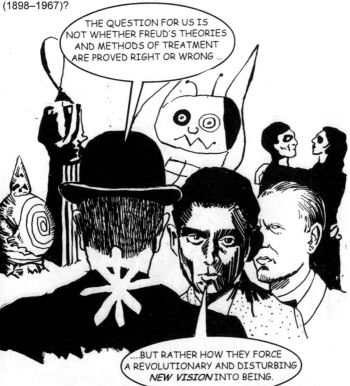

Not just through scientific and empirical proof, but through a complex articulation of mythology and poetics, Freud's compelling narratives – such as the case histories of the Rat Man, Little Hans, Dora and others – work on symbolism and themes of memory, repression and resistance, and are, as such, themselves superlative modernist masterpieces.

How Did Freud "Filter Through"?

How Freud was received by countless artists, writers, philosophers and musicians differed sharply according to selective needs. Some, such as the English novelist D.H. Lawrence, took up some of Freud's ideas only fitfully and then in an idiosyncratic way, using the discoveries of psychoanalysis to delve deep into issues of sexuality.

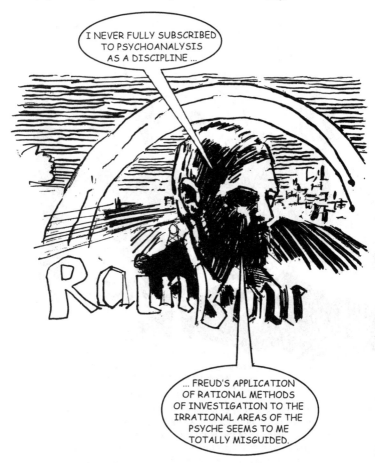

I NEVER FULLY SUBSCRIBED TO PSYCHOANALYSIS AS A DISCIPLINE ...

... FREUD'S APPLICATION OF RATIONAL METHODS OF INVESTIGATION TO THE IRRATIONAL AREAS OF THE PSYCHE SEEMS TO ME TOTALLY MISGUIDED.

The method of so-called "stream of consciousness" employed by
Dorothy Richardson (1873–1957) in her sprawling 13-volume novel
Pilgrimage (1915–38) and by James Joyce in the iconic *Ulysses* (1922)
is, to some degree, indebted to Freudian ideas about the way in which
the unconscious mind yokes together disparate images and feelings.

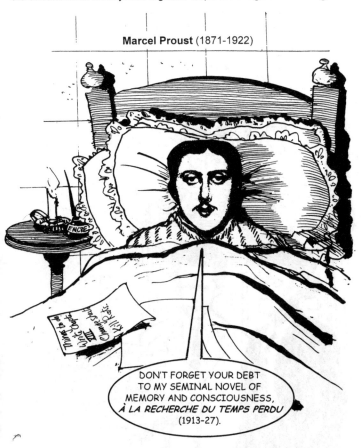

Marcel Proust (1871-1922)

DON'T FORGET YOUR DEBT
TO MY SEMINAL NOVEL OF
MEMORY AND CONSCIOUSNESS,
À LA RECHERCHE DU TEMPS PERDU
(1913-27).

"Stream of consciousness" exposes the deep self of a character – what
Virginia Woolf celebrated as "the dark places of psychology". It has now
become a commonplace feature in novel-writing.

The Century's Greatest Listener …

Although "stream of consciousness" – a phrase coined by the psychologist **William James** (1842–1910) – is a technique commonly ascribed to novel-writing, other art forms adopted the psychoanalytic perspective. **Sergei Eisenstein** (1898–1948), the Russian film-maker, discussed with James Joyce the possibility of working on a cinema project.

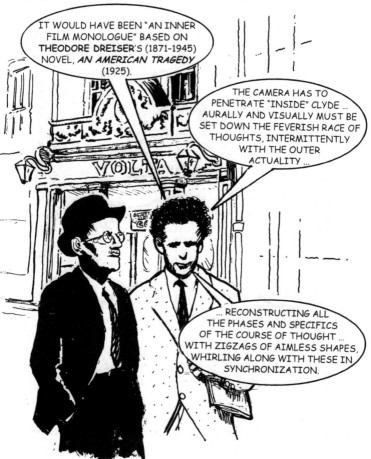

IT WOULD HAVE BEEN "AN INNER FILM MONOLOGUE" BASED ON THEODORE DREISER'S (1871-1945) NOVEL, *AN AMERICAN TRAGEDY* (1925).

THE CAMERA HAS TO PENETRATE "INSIDE" CLYDE … AURALLY AND VISUALLY MUST BE SET DOWN THE FEVERISH RACE OF THOUGHTS, INTERMITTENTLY WITH THE OUTER ACTUALITY …

… RECONSTRUCTING ALL THE PHASES AND SPECIFICS OF THE COURSE OF THOUGHT … WITH ZIGZAGS OF AIMLESS SHAPES, WHIRLING ALONG WITH THESE IN SYNCHRONIZATION.

It is almost impossible to quantify the influence that Freud exerted, even just in the cultural domain. When Freud died in 1939, in exile in London after his escape from Nazi Austria, W.H. Auden paid tribute to "his technique of unsettlement".

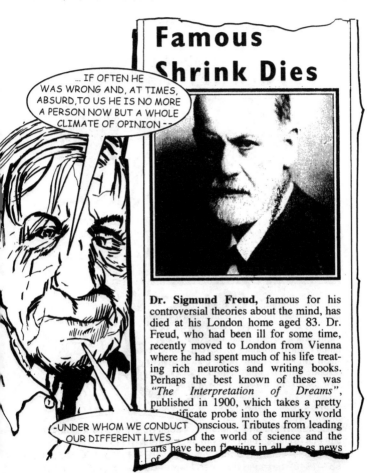

Psychoanalysis and Surrealism

But it was one specific movement, **Surrealism**, which explicitly and wholeheartedly embraced the ideas of Freud for its own creative ends.

Dada, which originated in Zurich in 1916, was a forerunner of Surrealism.

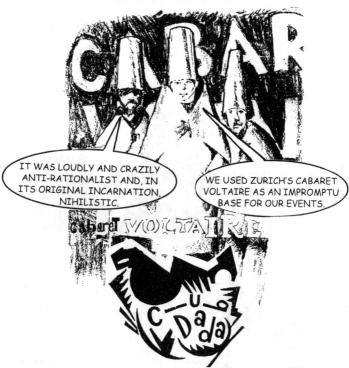

IT WAS LOUDLY AND CRAZILY ANTI-RATIONALIST AND, IN ITS ORIGINAL INCARNATION, NIHILISTIC.

WE USED ZURICH'S CABARET VOLTAIRE AS AN IMPROMPTU BASE FOR OUR EVENTS.

Among its members and fellow travellers were the artists **Max Ernst** (1891–1976), based in Cologne, and **Hans Arp** (1886–1966), **Tristan Tzara** (1896–1963), **Francis Picabia** (1879–1953) and **Kurt Schwitters** (1887–1948), based in Hanover. **Marcel Duchamp** (1887–1968), although not formally a Dadaist, was a kindred spirit. His famous "ready-mades" – the urinal, bottle-rack and other "found objects" – posed the question of what constituted art.

Generally speaking, Dada was a-political or nihilistic, but **Berlin Dada** had a more political agenda. Some of its members had links to the German Communist Party (KPD), and it became the breeding ground for several artists who would flourish in the next decades.

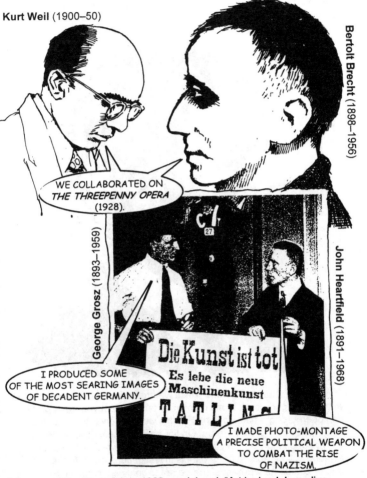

A banner at the Dada fair in 1922 proclaimed: "Art is dead. Long live the new machine art of Tatlin!"

The Birth of Surrealism by Manifesto

Many Dadaists subsequently converted to Surrealism. And it was with Surrealism that the psychoanalytic turn became explicit. But Surrealism was officially constituted in 1924 by André Breton in Paris. It came into being by manifesto …

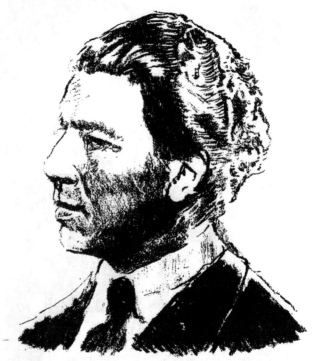

"… a part of our mental world which we pretended not to be concerned with any longer – and, in my opinion by far the most important part – has been brought back to light. For this we must give thanks to the discoveries of Sigmund Freud. On the basis of these discoveries a current of opinion is finally forming by means of which the human explorer will be able to carry out his investigations much further, authorized as he will henceforth be not to confine himself solely to the most summary realities. The imagination is perhaps on the point of reasserting itself, of reclaiming its rights."

This manifesto embodies many of the themes and issues which were to preoccupy the Surrealists.

The "mental world": they were constantly fascinated by psychology and the insights this could throw on the everyday world – in particular, the unconscious and all its attributes as analysed by Freud, which Breton highlights.

The "explorer": the idea of the artist investigating virgin territory and the primeval core of being, but also hinting at the connections with ethnography.

And, above all, the promotion of the **Imagination** against the dictates of reason.

This manifesto also contains a paradoxical aspect of Surrealism – its need to look for "authorization".

I WILL EXCOMMUNICATE - AS IF FROM A *RELIGION* - THOSE ARTISTS AND WRITERS WHO DIVERGE FROM ITS RULES!

BRETON WAS ALWAYS EXTREMELY CAREFUL TO POLICE OUR ACTIVITIES AND DECLARATIONS.

"The Impossible Dream"

There was an extraordinary "wager" in the programme of the Surrealists, and one which, in the end, they were unable to fulfil.

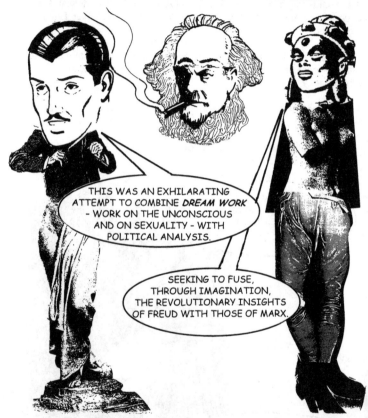

THIS WAS AN EXHILARATING ATTEMPT TO COMBINE *DREAM WORK* – WORK ON THE UNCONSCIOUS AND ON SEXUALITY – WITH POLITICAL ANALYSIS.

SEEKING TO FUSE, THROUGH IMAGINATION, THE REVOLUTIONARY INSIGHTS OF FREUD WITH THOSE OF MARX.

So it was not just a question of appropriating Freudian symbols and images – the Oedipus figure, for example – but of working *on* the texts of the unconscious. And this entailed a political dimension – to explore not only their own dreams but also the collective dreams and myths of society, transgressing the surface of reality to discover authentic latent meanings.

Some of the most powerful and disturbing ventures into the "socially transgressive" were undertaken by **Antonin Artaud** (1896–1948). His **Theatre of Cruelty** (1938) was designed as a pestilential and delirious exorcism of social demons.

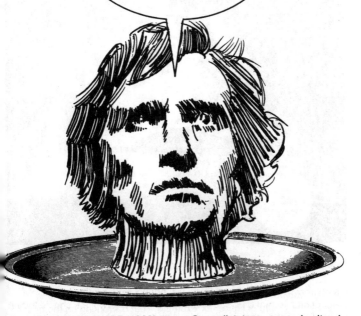

IF THE ESSENCE OF THEATRE IS LIKE THE PLAGUE, THIS IS NOT BECAUSE IT IS CONTAGIOUS, BUT BECAUSE LIKE THE PLAGUE IT'S THE REVELATION, THE PUTTING FORWARD, THE EXTERIORIZATION OF THE DEEP LATENT CRUELTY THAT ALL THE PERVERSE POTENTIALITY OF THE SPIRIT PLACES ON AN INDIVIDUAL OR A PEOPLE ...

Georges Bataille (1897–1962), an ex-Surrealist, transgressed cultural taboos with his brew of pornography, philosophy and ethnography. He invented a "College of Sacred Sociology" which performed deviant Surrealist researches of great interest today.

"Surreal" has now become a household adjective. We commonly use it to signify anything incongruous or bizarre.

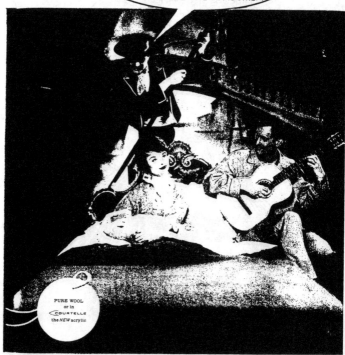

Dream of luxury—and double it

It's an irony that the original Surrealist project to revolutionize our perceptions, to make us see ordinary things in a new light, should today be applied to the most mercantile methods of the consumer society. Perhaps we should rewrite the 19th-century dictum that "all art constantly aspires towards the condition of music" to read, "all the modernist arts aspire towards the condition of advertising".

A number of Surrealist films were directly inspired by psychoanalysis. The partnership of Luis Buñuel and Salvador Dalí was to produce two of the most famous of these: *Un Chien Andalou* (1928) and *L'Age d'Or* (1932).

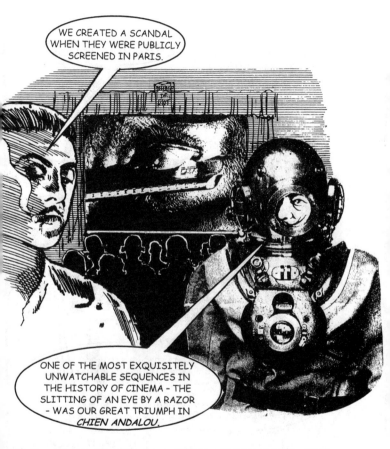

The Sea-Shell and the Clergyman (1927) by **Germaine Dulac** (1882–1942), with Antonin Artaud as scriptwriter, is another surreal vision which combines the bizarre and the everyday within the narrative of a chase.

The "Dream Factory"

But it is not only in explicitly Surrealist films that strange dream-like narratives of the unconscious occur. Even films made in the commercial "dream factory" of Hollywood often have a surreal edge. All kinds of cinema genres lend themselves to the surreal treatment ...

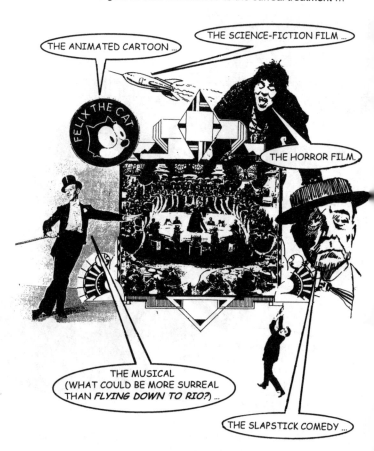

Not by chance, film is often compared to dream. Through close-ups, montage and the whole gamut of ordinary, special and extraordinary effects, film is able to delve deep beyond its mimetic surface. **Walter Benjamin** (1892–1940) made the parallels clear in "The Work of Art in the Age of Mechanical Reproduction" (1936).

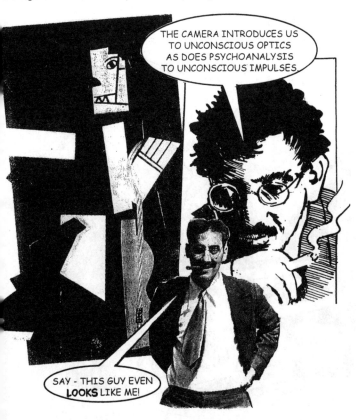

He also rightly pointed out that ideas which baffled the uninformed spectator in a Dadaist piece of work (he could just as well have been referring to other "difficult" modernist art) would be immediately understood in the medium of cinema. Charlie Chaplin and Groucho Marx are "Dadaist" in their comedies.

What is the Role of the City in Modernism?

Modernity and modernism are centrally located in urban culture and the great capital cities – Paris (3 million), London (5 million), Berlin (2 million) and New York (5 million). In the years preceding the First World War, these were to experience exponential growth, economically and demographically.

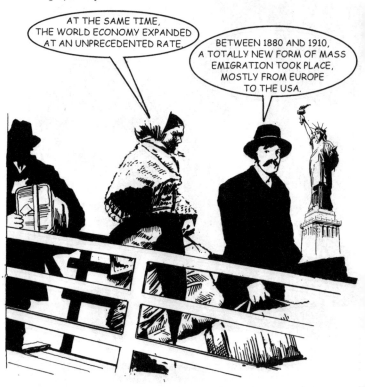

These developments gave birth to industrialized mass societies hungry for every form of consumer item, fashion and entertainment. Fuelled by social aspirations and desires, these new masses indulged in "conspicuous consumption" (one way that the better-off could signal their material success and social status).

The Crowd

The city crowd was both an anonymous phenomenon in which the individual could hide, and the place where identity (crucially, at times *political* identity) could be invented. The crowd became a key image of the conflicting values associated with the modern urban environment.

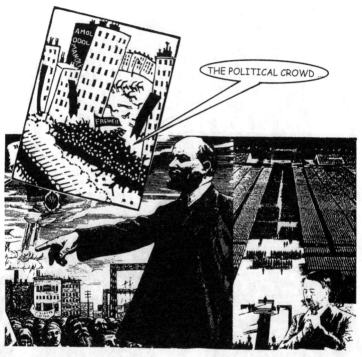

The revolutionary crowd harangued by Lenin or Trotsky in 1917.

The mass disciplined ranks of Hitler worship at the Nazi Nuremberg Rallies of 1933.

The crowd as chaotic exuberance, as depicted in **King Vidor**'s (1894–1982) film *The Crowd* (1928), or at the end of **Marcel Carné**'s (1900–96) *Les Enfants du Paradis* (1945).

The Human River …

The crowd was a potent symbol of the compacted mass of urban humanity and of history "on the march". It provided an evocative passage in T.S. Eliot's *The Waste Land* …

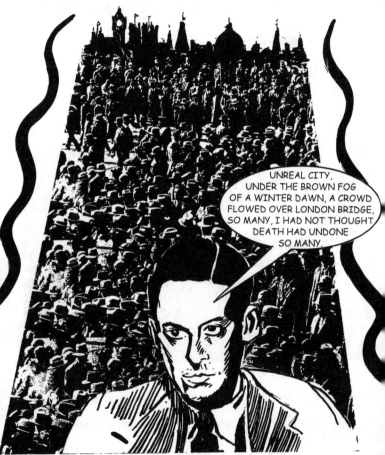

The crowd flows, adopts the movement of the river which it is crossing – as if the very essence of the city had been given over to natural, inevitable forces.

... and the *Flâneur*

Charles Baudelaire (1821–67) inaugurated the key figure of the urban *flâneur* or stroller in his writings. The *flâneur* was a "hero" of modern life, a participant observer ...

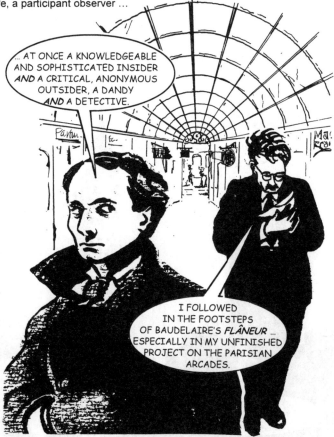

For Benjamin, the lure and fascination of modern city life lay in its surface narratives, the ephemeral, the fugitive, the new. Running through the centre of the Paris metropolis, the new glass-covered arcades or "passages" were marvellous metaphors for urban display and consumption: private and public, inside and outside.

The City as Narrative

Modernist arts are unimaginable without the city. Whether as backdrop or central protagonist, it is rare not to find a real or imaginary city present in a novel or film. Cities are the very stuff of key modernist novels such as **Louis Aragon**'s (1897–1982) *Paris Peasant* (1926), **John Dos Passos**'s (1896–1970) *Manhattan Transfer* (1925), **Alfred Döblin**'s (1878–1957) *Berlin Alexanderplatz* (1929), James Joyce's *Ulysses* (1922). The list is endless.

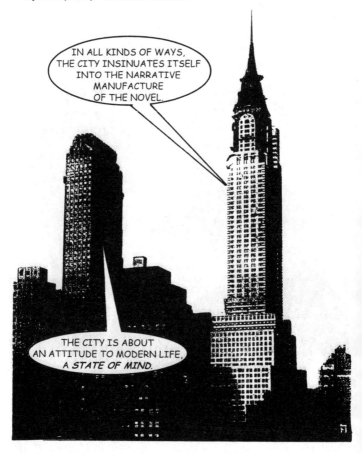

The simultaneous levels of different activities, intersecting itineraries and modes of transport, fortuitous encounters between people and things, provided films with instant photogenic plots and stories.

Fritz Lang's (1890–1976) *Metropolis* (1926) and *M* (1931) are two well-known films which exploit the expressive and dramatic potential of the city. In more experimental vein, **Dziga Vertov**'s (1896–1954) *The Man With a Movie Camera* (1929) and **Walter Ruttman**'s (1887–1941) *Berlin, Symphony of a City* (1927) explore the poetic everyday of the city.

METROPOLIS

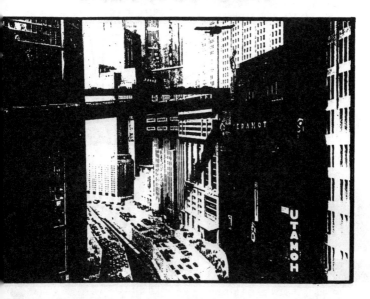

Hollywood produced countless films which used the urban landscape. The "*film noir*" genre in particular explored memorably the dark corners and violent streets of a dystopian America.

Architects' Utopia

The city could also function as utopian map. The Futurist architect
Antonio Sant'Elia (1888–1916) designed (though never actually built)
his grand visions of the city. The influential German school of design,
the **Bauhaus**, was founded by architects **Walter Gropius** (1883–1969)
– its director from 1919 to 1928 – and **Ludwig Mies van der Rohe**
(1886–1969).

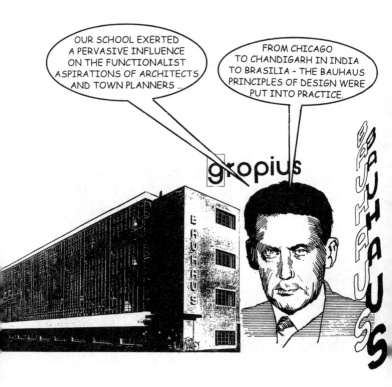

Sometimes it is difficult to distinguish between utopia and dystopia. The
exhilarating urban panoramas of Sant'Elia seem so similar to the sense
of nightmare in Lang's film *Metropolis*.

But if there is one name which conjures up the attempt, however misguided, to create utopian visions of buildings and cities, it is the controversial **Le Corbusier** (1887–1965). His concept of the house as "a machine to live in" was extended to the city, whose streets were to become "machines for traffic".

His utopian designs for the future have now become associated with a discredited modernist dream, our contemporary urban dystopia.

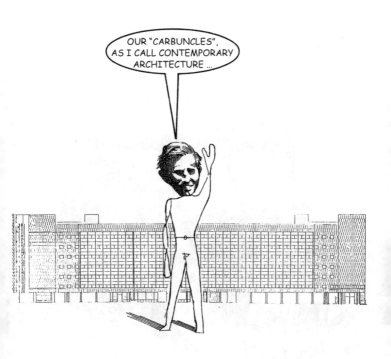

Le Corbusier's vision was a rendering of the city which banished the unpredictable and the deviant: "Nothing is contradictory any more. Everything is in its place, properly arranged in order and hierarchy."

Why Are Modernists So Often "Exiles"?

The city acts as a centripetal force in modernism, drawing into itself talent and energy. The great capital cities of Europe offered "asylum" to these modernist emigrants. Many were exiles in their own land, class immigrants (such as the Cubist painter Braque) who had their roots in the provinces and discovered the great capital cities.

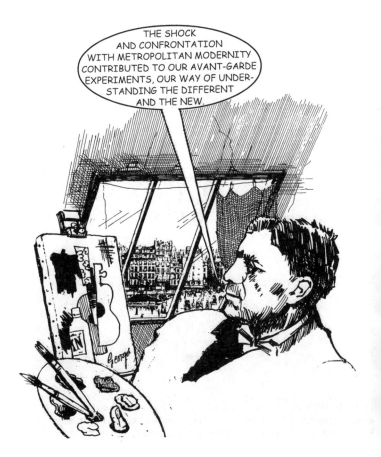

Imitating the mass emigrations in microcosm, there were also those who opted to change countries. A great number of prominent modernists were in fact such "exiles" by choice. Picasso and **Juan Gris** (1887–1927) were Spaniards who went to live in France. Ezra Pound, T.S. Eliot and the Imagist poet **H.D.** (Hilda Doolittle, 1886–1961) left the United States to live in England.

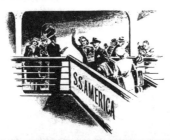

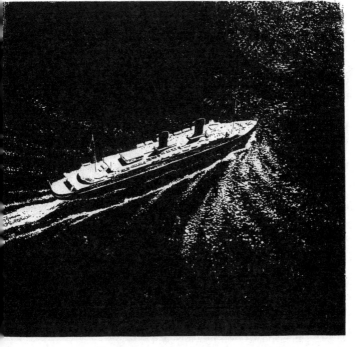

Modernist Nomads

The "lost generation" of American expatriates – **Ernest Hemingway** (1899–1961), **F. Scott Fitzgerald** (1896–1940) and Gertrude Stein – flirted with exile in Europe and Paris.

The exemplary exile is James Joyce, who deliberately turned his back on Ireland.

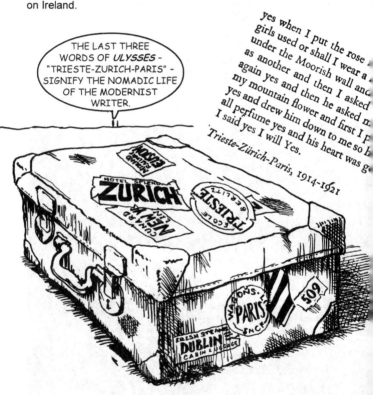

THE LAST THREE WORDS OF *ULYSSES* – "TRIESTE-ZURICH-PARIS" – SIGNIFY THE NOMADIC LIFE OF THE MODERNIST WRITER.

yes when I put the rose in my hair like the Andalusian girls used or shall I wear a red yes and how he kissed me under the Moorish wall and I thought well as well him as another and then I asked him with my eyes to ask again yes and then he asked me would I yes to say yes my mountain flower and first I put my arms around him yes and drew him down to me so he could feel my breasts all perfume yes and his heart was going like mad and yes I said yes I will Yes.

Trieste-Zürich-Paris, 1914–1921

Guillaume Apollinaire came originally from Poland. Blaise Cendrars left Switzerland to roam adventurously in China, Persia and the Americas, finally settling in Paris. D.H. Lawrence escaped the stultifying confines of 1920s England to travel in Europe and Mexico.

How often we discover Paris as the final location in a journey. Paris drew artists and writers like a magnet. Indeed, one could narrate an account of the "heroic" or early period of modernism by writing the cultural history of Paris during the first 30 years of the 20th century.

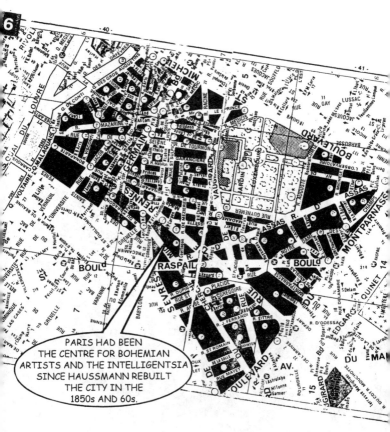

PARIS HAD BEEN THE CENTRE FOR BOHEMIAN ARTISTS AND THE INTELLIGENTSIA SINCE HAUSSMANN REBUILT THE CITY IN THE 1850s AND 60s.

Paris is almost "spiritually" evoked in one of the greatest of all (pre-) modernist novels, *The Ambassadors*, written in 1903 by Henry James. All of James's work is concerned with exploring the double-edged fascination that Europe, the old country, held over the brash and mercantile, the dynamic and optimistic Americans.

Paris would remain the pre-eminent metropolis until the 1940s and 50s, when New York took over as the foremost cultural capital of the world. Leading up to the Second World War, the direction was from the envenomed shores of Europe to the USA. **W.H. Auden** (1907–73) and **Christopher Isherwood** (1904–86) notoriously left the stricken shores of England. Hundreds of German Jewish and anti-Fascist artists, writers and film-makers also headed for the USA in the 1930s. The reasons for exile are various.

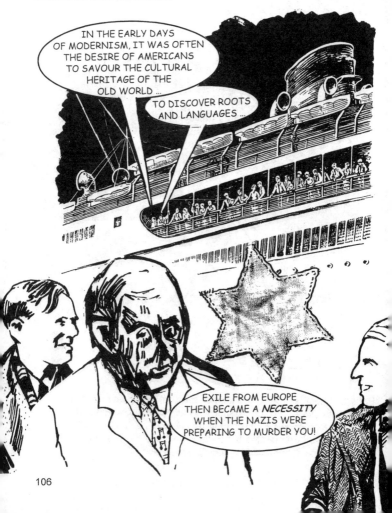

IN THE EARLY DAYS OF MODERNISM, IT WAS OFTEN THE DESIRE OF AMERICANS TO SAVOUR THE CULTURAL HERITAGE OF THE OLD WORLD ...

TO DISCOVER ROOTS AND LANGUAGES ...

EXILE FROM EUROPE THEN BECAME A *NECESSITY* WHEN THE NAZIS WERE PREPARING TO MURDER YOU!

The great novels of Henry James, from *Portrait of a Lady* to *The Ambassadors*, were centrally concerned with exploring the conflicts and consolations which Europe held for an American sensibility; for Ezra Pound, it was the pleasure of immersing himself in the world of Provençal and troubadour poetry; for T.S. Eliot, to make contact with the traces of a world which existed before the industrial revolution and the machine age, a time when, as in the 17th century, there was a fusion of culture and community (or so he believed and argued). Eliot had studied Greek and Latin at Harvard, and read in Italian, French and German; his early poetic infatuation was with Jules Laforgue, the French "decadent" poet born in Montevideo, Uruguay.

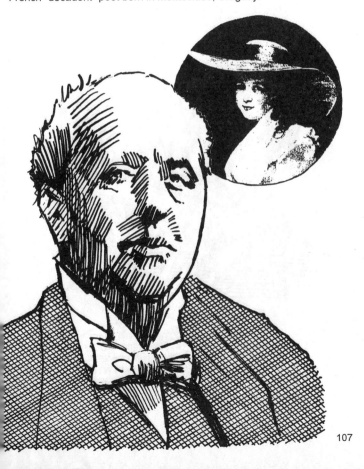

Exile Into Language

Exile can take geographic form. At other times, linguistic. Or sometimes the two together. It has often been remarked that Joseph Conrad's precise and deep way with English was due to the fact that he learnt it as a third language after Polish and French.

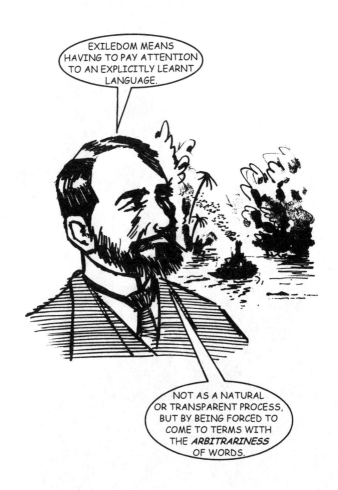

Women writers, interested in exploring the intrusions of modernity on consciousness, functioned in another kind of "linguistic exile". Writers such as Dorothy Richardson and Virginia Woolf in England, and the American Gertrude Stein (living in France and doubly exiled through geography and masculine language), are good examples.

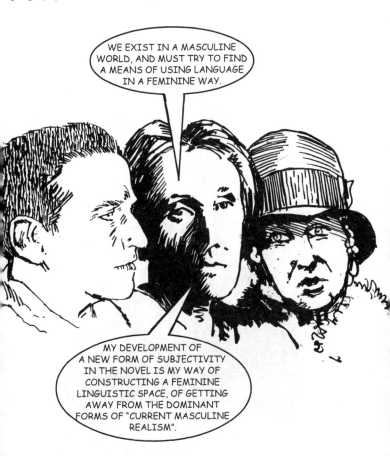

As Gertrude Stein put it in an interview towards the end of her life, perhaps she was far too alienated from the masculine writing of the past.

"You see it is the people who generally smell of the museums who are accepted, and it is the new who are not accepted. You have got to accept a complete difference. It is hard to accept that, it is much easier to have one hand in the past. That is why James Joyce was accepted and I was not. He leaned toward the past, in my work the newness and difference is fundamental."

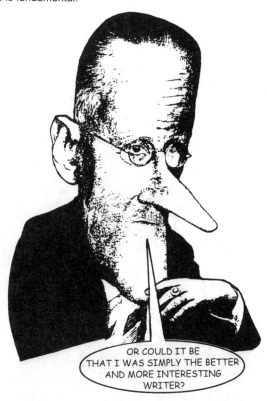

What is the Role of Élites and Avant-gardes in Modernism?

The problem of élites is obsessional in early modernity. Nordau's psychiatric analysis was chiefly concerned with a "social prophylaxis" to safeguard a progressive European élite from contamination by decadence. The sociology of **Vilfredo Pareto** (1848–1923), **Gaetano Mosca** (1858–1941), **Max Weber** (1864–1920) and others is focused on the problem of élites and their function in society.

An élite "tactical force" was central to Lenin's thinking, and widespread among anarchists, Narodnik terrorists and other political theorists like **Georges Sorel** (1847–1922), both left and right.

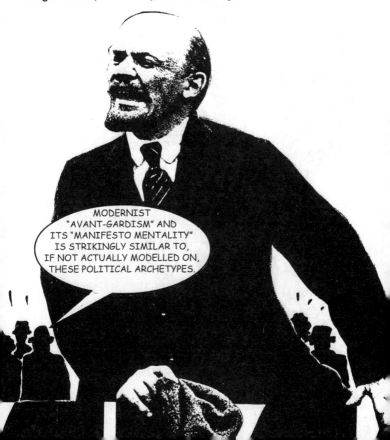

MODERNIST "AVANT-GARDISM" AND ITS "MANIFESTO MENTALITY" IS STRIKINGLY SIMILAR TO, IF NOT ACTUALLY MODELLED ON, THESE POLITICAL ARCHETYPES.

Is Avant-gardism "Pure" Modernism?

The term **avant-garde** is often associated with modernism. For many commentators, the various avant-garde movements *are* modernism. They represent modernism's project in its purest and most vibrant form. But we may find the contrast between the specifics of the avant-gardes (at the cutting edge of culture at specific historical moments) and modernism (describing a more general tendency) helpful in enabling us to situate a writer such as Ernest Hemingway.

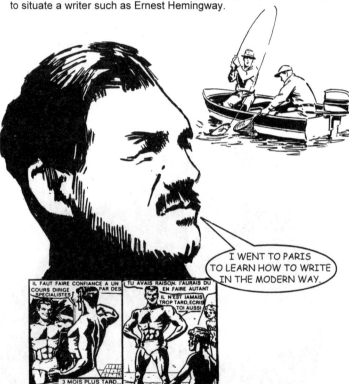

I WENT TO PARIS TO LEARN HOW TO WRITE IN THE MODERN WAY.

He can usefully be described as a modernist writer, insofar as modernism is understood to be a "structure of feeling", but not associated with an avant-garde positioned in relation to theoretical statements.

Avant-garde is a French military term which referred to advance or "shock" troops. It was first used metaphorically in 19th-century France to designate artistic movements "ahead" of received ideas and traditions. The military metaphor has its drawbacks.

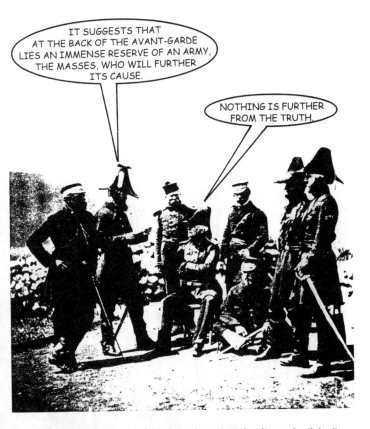

The avant-garde is successful only to the extent that its credentials, its cutting-edge status, are not in doubt. The moment that a style or an attitude becomes accepted and commonplace, that art is over. The war against mass impoverished sensibilities is lost.

The Cohesion of Avant-gardes

The avant-garde does resemble a military formation in other respects. It constructs and maintains a "corporate" identity, it formulates a set of tactics and implements manoeuvres. Even with the most subversive avant-garde group, there is a group sense of belonging. Artists and writers fall in and out, but share – at least initially – a common set of aims with which they are happy to associate themselves.

Being a founding member is crucial. It is difficult to join halfway through a movement. **William Empson** (1906–84), the English poet and critic, writing of his admiration for the 1930s poetry of Auden and its distinctive tone of voice, comments …

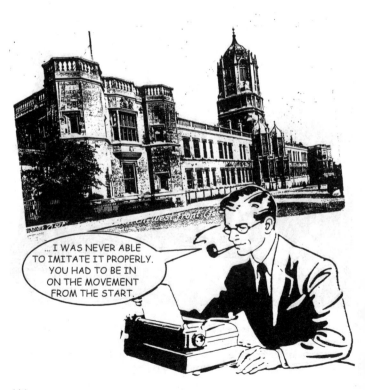

… I WAS NEVER ABLE TO IMITATE IT PROPERLY. YOU HAD TO BE IN ON THE MOVEMENT FROM THE START.

Perhaps in our "*recherche du temps perdu*" we fictionalize and build imaginary narratives of shared endeavours, stolen kisses and ideals merely on the basis of a few photographs taken outside a Montparnasse café, the Dome perhaps. **Paul Eluard** (1895–1952) drapes an arm over Picasso and his lover Dora Maar. James Joyce, **Ford Madox Ford** (1873–1939) and Sylvia Beach pose outside the Left Bank bookshop, Shakespeare and Company.

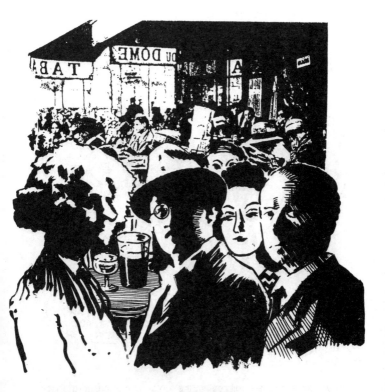

Indisputably, there were some exceptional bondings: for example, the creative friendship of Ezra Pound and T.S. Eliot, or Picasso and Braque who for a time shared a vision of Cubism.

Picasso's Alliances

Indeed, it is astonishing how often, for all his self-confidence, Picasso is seen as paired off with some other creative person (if it isn't with a new wife or lover). It's almost as if he were constructing for posterity a narrative of reflected glories: Picasso *and* Apollinaire, Picasso *and* Gertrude Stein, Picasso *and* Eluard (here the ties were political – the French Communist Party – as well as artistic). These corporate twinnings are a measure of Picasso's promotional charisma.

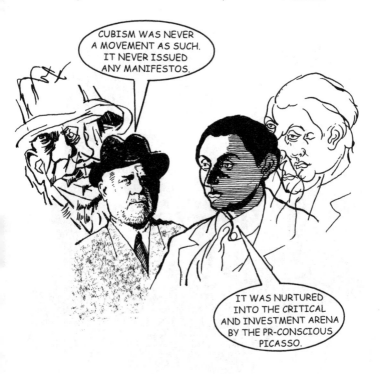

CUBISM WAS NEVER A MOVEMENT AS SUCH. IT NEVER ISSUED ANY MANIFESTOS.

IT WAS NURTURED INTO THE CRITICAL AND INVESTMENT ARENA BY THE PR-CONSCIOUS PICASSO.

What Clement Greenberg called the "golden umbilical cord" that attached the supposedly subversive avant-garde to the patrons, gallery owners and wealthy collectors was always well oiled by Picasso with his genius for self-publicity and promotion.

But were these creative friendships and groupings anything particularly new? One of the distinctive ways in which modernists articulated their sense of belonging (in opposition to the complacent world of the bourgeoisie or the ignorance of the working class) was through publishing manifestos and holding public events.

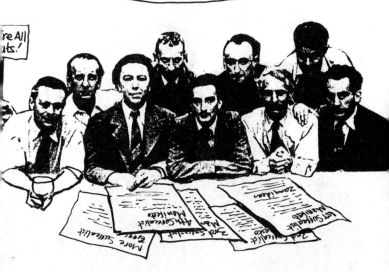

Some avant-garde groups had a free and easy membership. Others, such as the Surrealists, under the heavy hand of the French poet and polemicist André Breton, existed under threat of excommunication if they so much as strayed from the *diktat* of a manifesto. (This happened to Salvador Dalí.)

What Politics Did the Modernists Espouse?

The modernists were convinced – and sounded convincing – in their declarations and manifestos that they had something new to offer, that this newness was what made them artists and set them apart from others.

Ezra Pound's dictum expresses this sense of the avant-garde …

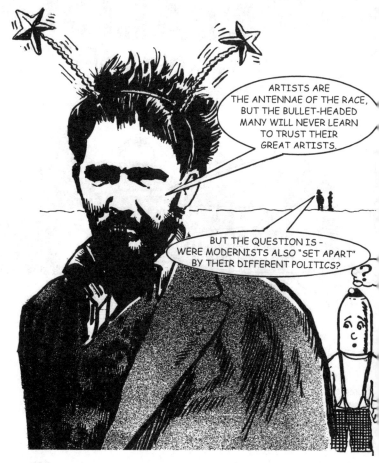

ARTISTS ARE THE ANTENNAE OF THE RACE, BUT THE BULLET-HEADED MANY WILL NEVER LEARN TO TRUST THEIR GREAT ARTISTS.

BUT THE QUESTION IS – WERE MODERNISTS ALSO "SET APART" BY THEIR DIFFERENT POLITICS?

One of the most exciting cultural phenomena occurred when the artistic avant-garde coincided with the political avant-garde. This happened spectacularly in the period of revolutionary Russia, before experimentalist activity was cut down by Stalin's cultural commissars of "Socialist Realism".

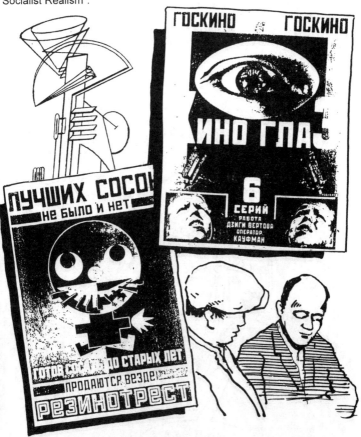

Artists' collectives such as **VKhUTEMAS** ("Higher State Technical-Artistic Studios", 1920) and the film production group **Feks** ("Factory of the Eccentric Actor", 1921–9) had encouraged individual artists to produce collaborative work that was politically inspiring as well as creatively challenging.

Reactionary Modernism?

The political allegiances of modernists has always been a vexed
question, particularly when applied to modernist Anglo-American writers.
If modernism in its most generalized definition is about responding to
the newness of the modern world, about radical change and innovation,
it seems perverse that many of its greatest writers and some of its
artists seemed to possess reactionary views in the political arena.

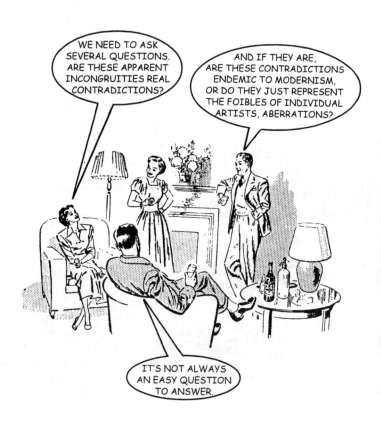

Recalling D.H. Lawrence's adage – "Never trust the artist. Trust the tale." – is important if we are to make sense of what seems to be at times the mistaken, misplaced or simply outrageous political attitudes of many canonical modernist writers and artists.

T.S. Eliot's anti-Semitism is notoriously instanced in reference to the lower case "jew" in the poem "Burbank with a Baedeker: Bleistein with a Cigar".

The rats are underneath the piles,
The jew is underneath the lot.
Money in furs …

This "lapsus" is compounded by a statement he made in a lecture in 1933 (hardly a date by which one can plead political innocence).

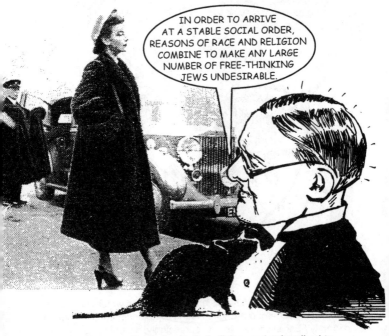

He had previously converted to Anglo-Catholicism and subscribed to the full regalia of conservative politics.

Modernists on the Ultra-Right

W.B. Yeats (1865–1939) had a more complex relationship to the politics of Ireland, although it is clear that his aristocratic infatuations were defiantly on the side of an Anglo-Irish Ascendancy in Ireland, and he flirted in the 1930s with the ultra-nationalist Irish Fascist movement.

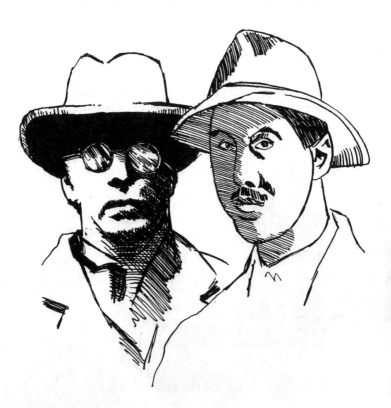

Wyndham Lewis (1882–1957), the painter and writer who led the Vorticist movement (an English blend of Futurism and Cubism), held defiantly Fascist views. Not too surprisingly, given their glorification of violence and machinic frenzy, many of the Futurists, including Marinetti, ended up siding with Mussolini.

The most notorious example of a modernist poet who went politically off the rails is Ezra Pound. Among poets writing in English, his work is held up along with Eliot's as the quintessence of the modernist spirit. But he was profoundly anti-Semitic and during the Second World War collaborated with the Italian Fascists in broadcasting fanatical statements to American troops over Rome Radio.

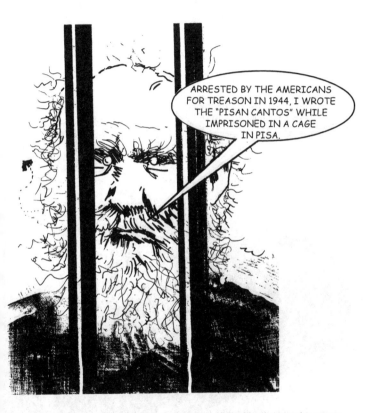

He was subsequently declared insane and spent the next twelve years in an asylum. This was a poet who was immersed in the culture of the medieval troubadours and Provençal poetry, the Chinese odes, Confucius and Japanese Noh theatre, the Greek poets and a whole range of other civilizations ...

The Political Errors of Modernism

We could list other modernists who veered to the extreme right.
Salvador Dalí returned to Spain after the Civil War and sided with
Franco's Fascist regime – to the disgust of his former Surrealist
colleague Buñuel. The French writer **Louis-Ferdinand Céline** (1894–
1961) espoused an obscene anti-Semitism and collaborated with the
Nazi Occupation, as did **Pierre Drieu la Rochelle** (1893–1945), who
committed suicide at the end of the war. As we shall see, their
experiences of the First World War – the lies, betrayals and futile
slaughter – had much to do with their decision.

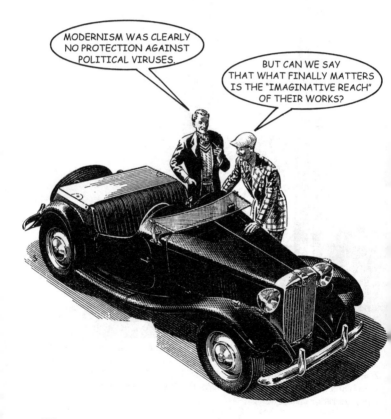

Of course, there were aberrations on the leftist side of the political divide. Duped writers and intellectuals persisted in defending Stalin at a time, in the 1930s, when his crimes against humanity were becoming public knowledge.

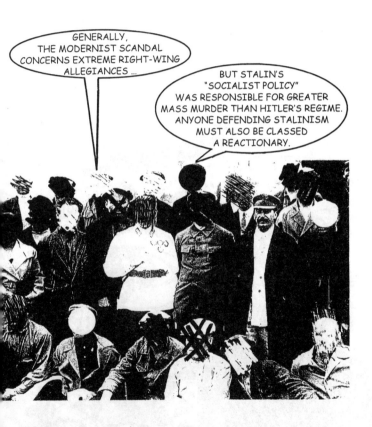

The paradox has become glaring by now. Modernists with ultra-right views are condemned as reactionary, but those with apparently leftist ones are condoned as "socially progressive". Reality is not so simple as that.

Examples of Progressive Modernists

Picasso identified briefly with the French Communist Party. His painting *Guernica* (1937) lent support to the anti-Franco resistance in Spain. Then there are all those committed writers and artists for whom innovation at a formal aesthetic level combined integrally with forward-thinking political ideas. This is especially true of the exemplary Russian artists and writers of the 1920s – before the years of Stalinist repression, **Zhdanovism** and Socialist Realism – such as **Kasimir Malevich** (1878–1935), **Aleksandr Rodchenko** (1891–1956), El Lissitzky, Tatlin, **Vladimir Mayakovsky** (1893–1930) and **Vsevelod Meyerhold** (1874–1940).

We have already mentioned the German dramatist and poet, Bertolt Brecht.

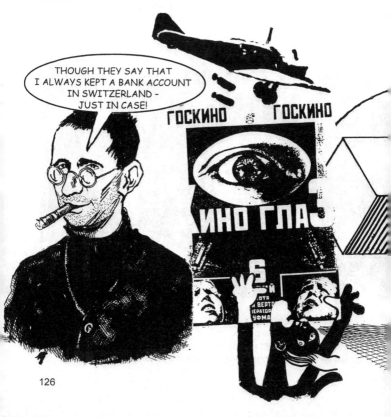

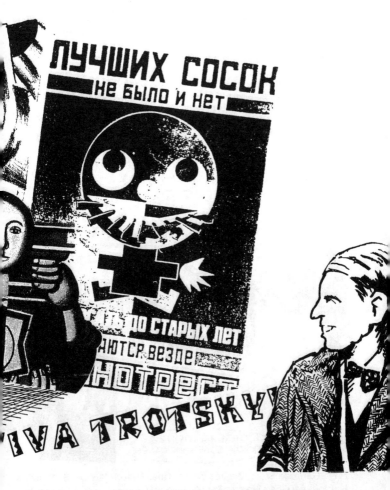

W.H. Auden was a leftist, at least until he emigrated to the United States. Fernand Léger was a committed Marxist painter of lyrical machines interlaced with revolutionary bodies. **Diego Rivera** (1886–1957), the Mexican muralist, espoused Trotskyist Communism.

No One's Perfect …

It should be noted that among modernists and critics of modernity there is probably a preponderance of progressive views. There are the exceptions, of course – major figures such as Heidegger. And even those with left-wing politics were not always that "correct".

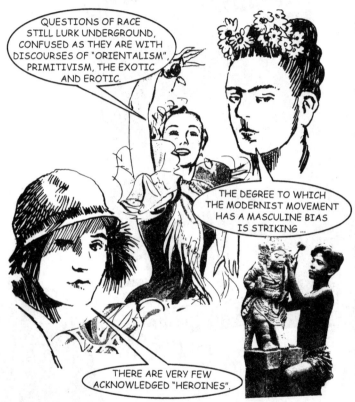

QUESTIONS OF RACE STILL LURK UNDERGROUND, CONFUSED AS THEY ARE WITH DISCOURSES OF "ORIENTALISM", PRIMITIVISM, THE EXOTIC AND EROTIC.

THE DEGREE TO WHICH THE MODERNIST MOVEMENT HAS A MASCULINE BIAS IS STRIKING …

THERE ARE VERY FEW ACKNOWLEDGED "HEROINES".

H.D., Gertrude Stein, Virginia Woolf, **Tina Modotti** (1896–1942); **Frida Kahlo** (1910–54); **Marina Tsvetayeva** (1892–1941) … Gender and race were to be glaring blind spots and omissions in much modernist practice. The growth of feminism and of post-colonial theory have been attempts to deal with these, even as they operated within the mainstream of progressive ideologies.

How Does Modernism Relate to Mass Culture?

Modernism's élitism, avant-gardism and politics stand in a complex and thorny relation to mass culture. Understanding that relationship will help to clarify the question of modernism's "reaction against" modernity.

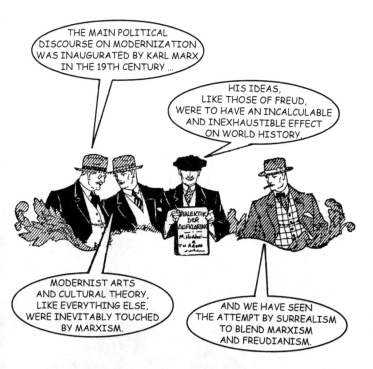

THE MAIN POLITICAL DISCOURSE ON MODERNIZATION WAS INAUGURATED BY KARL MARX IN THE 19TH CENTURY ...

HIS IDEAS, LIKE THOSE OF FREUD, WERE TO HAVE AN INCALCULABLE AND INEXHAUSTIBLE EFFECT ON WORLD HISTORY.

MODERNIST ARTS AND CULTURAL THEORY, LIKE EVERYTHING ELSE, WERE INEVITABLY TOUCHED BY MARXISM.

AND WE HAVE SEEN THE ATTEMPT BY SURREALISM TO BLEND MARXISM AND FREUDIANISM.

The **Frankfurt School** was one influential grouping which drew its inspiration from the teachings of Marx and Freud. It was set up in 1924 and included the aesthetician and philosopher **Theodor Adorno** (1903–69), the political thinker **Herbert Marcuse** (1898–1979) and, in an unofficial capacity, Walter Benjamin. The group fled to New York when the Nazi Party came to power in 1933, but its reflections on an advanced politics, via the detour of art and culture, remain unavoidable reference points in mapping out modernism's impact on modern life.

Against Mass Culture

Adorno championed the avant-garde, especially in music – the 12-tone serialism of **Arnold Schoenberg** (1874–1951) and **Alban Berg** (1885–1935). This led him at times into complicated terrain.

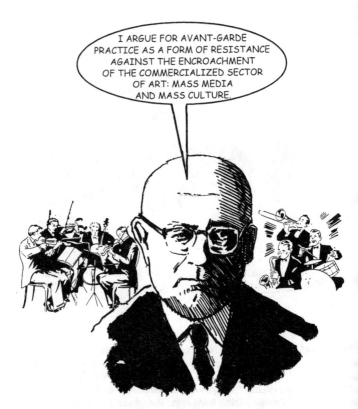

I ARGUE FOR AVANT-GARDE PRACTICE AS A FORM OF RESISTANCE AGAINST THE ENCROACHMENT OF THE COMMERCIALIZED SECTOR OF ART: MASS MEDIA AND MASS CULTURE.

His aesthetic arguments are complex. But although he was not upholding "élitism" in a simplistic fashion, his bias involved him in denouncing "primitive" music forms such as jazz.

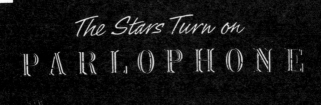

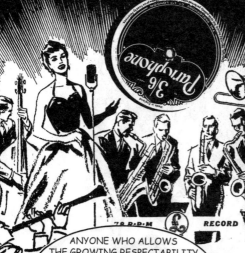

131

Understanding Mass Culture

Walter Benjamin had a more positive attitude to mass culture, although like Adorno his views were complex and nuanced. He thought and wrote about art in the 20th century with an acuity and suggestiveness which remain compelling to this day. Indeed, he enables us to take critical positions on the ideological values of modernist work and movements. His essays "The Work of Art in the Age of Mechanical Reproduction" (1936) and "The Author as Producer" (1934) are seminal to the cultural politics of the 1930s.

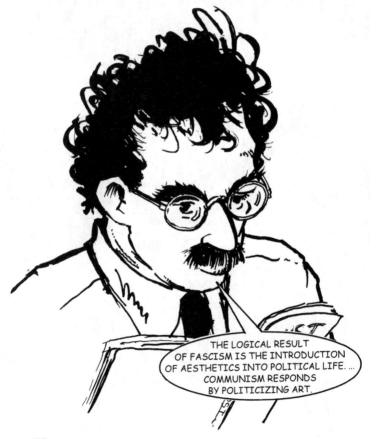

THE LOGICAL RESULT OF FASCISM IS THE INTRODUCTION OF AESTHETICS INTO POLITICAL LIFE. ... COMMUNISM RESPONDS BY POLITICIZING ART.

We can focus on modernist works themselves and try to discover what exactly is being articulated in those imaginary spaces that are defined by the words (or brush-strokes or sounds) and in the mind of the reader (or spectator or listener).

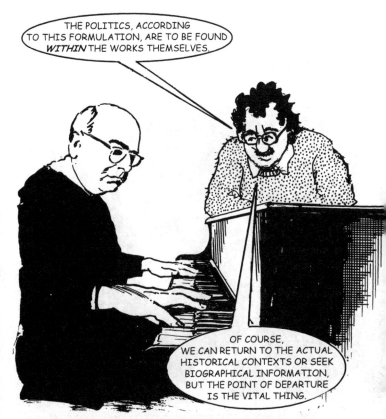

The question of the politics of modernism was understood from the beginning to be an important issue in clarifying what modernism represented. Sometimes even its denial (such as with the Bloomsbury group and Virginia Woolf) and the elevation of "art-for-art"-style rhetoric signified a political position.

Cultural Industries

Politics is an issue that has been addressed continuously by artists and critics. Some of the key debates are embedded in the fabric and history of modernism itself. For example, the thinking of the Frankfurt School on the relationship between aesthetics and politics constitutes an important strand of late modernism.

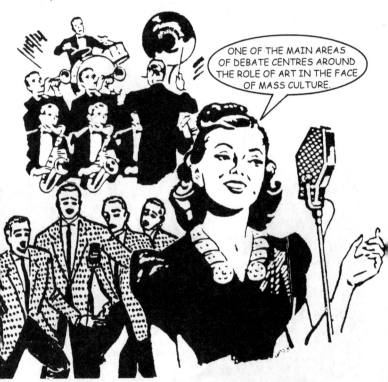

Mass culture's exponential growth through new technologies of reproduction and distribution – film and radio, mass circulation publications, photography, advertising – and the building up of what were later called "the consciousness industries" operated a real revolution in the way that people conducted their lives, their beliefs and their desires.

One attitude, as we noted with the early avant-garde Cubists and both the Italian and Russian Futurists, was to embrace the forces of modernization wholeheartedly.

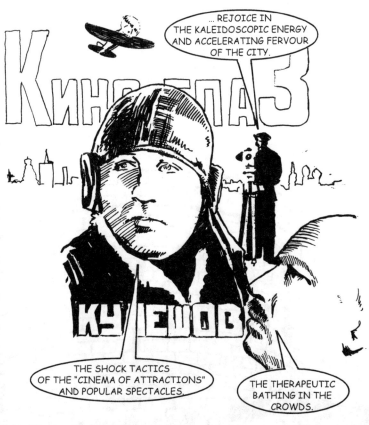

Art in this scenario should attempt to connect to this energy and find new ways with words and images, new structures of feeling.

The other attitude, exemplified in the conservative thinking of T.S. Eliot and others, was based on a pessimistic reading of modernization. Here, the urban environment bred solitariness, noise and anonymous crowds. Popular cinema was fodder for the masses.

The art that ensued from this interpretation of modernization could be seen as reactive and élitist, anti-democratic, and at odds with mass culture: art was valued not because it reflected or entered into a dynamic relationship with a changing world, but because it offered itself as the ultimate consolation, an imaginary cocoon. In the case of what Wyndham Lewis called "the men of 1914" (i.e., Pound, Eliot, Joyce and Lewis himself), the montage and collisions of words, allusions and quotations culled from different registers and cultures became the meaning of the work, rather than relating words to external reality. Clearly, this was not an attitude which was likely to lead to the production of popular and populist work.

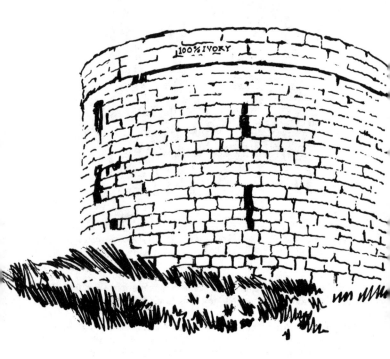

In 1928, **Arnold Bennett** (1837–1931), a popular novelist who wrote "sensible" stories with what E.M. Forster was to call "rounded characters", lambasted his modernist colleagues.

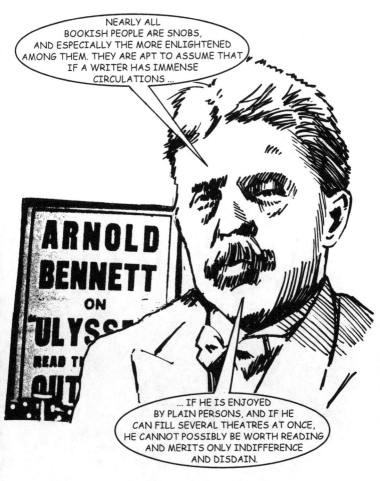

And this apparent disdain for the masses or mass culture was compounded by an unavoidable fact: the frequent difficulty (sometimes the excruciating difficulty) of much modernist work.

The Impact of the First World War

These difficulties can be partly explained by the impact of external events. An "inherent" reaction against modernity was exacerbated and became clearer as the socio-political situation grew darker during and after the First World War. This hugely traumatic event utterly changed people's sensibilities. Italian Futurists had sung the praises of war before European civilization attempted its own suicide …

"War is beautiful because it establishes man's dominion over the subjugated machinery by means of gas masks, terrifying megaphones, flame throwers, and small tanks. War is beautiful because it enriches a flowering meadow with the fiery orchids of machine guns. War is beautiful because it combines the gunfire, the cannonades, the cease-fire, the scents, and the stench of putrefaction into a symphony."

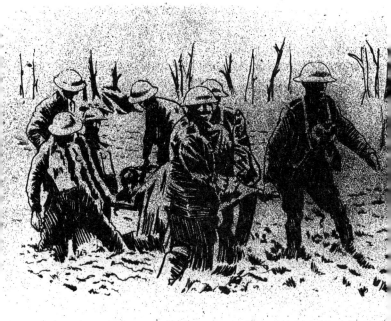

Such rhetoric was obscene in the face of actual carnage – an unparalleled slaughter of 8.5 million in trench warfare, 1914 to 1918. *"And for what?"* That, precisely, was the question that modernism had to pose itself. The official information propagated during the war had been brazen lies. Lies and "laughter out of dead bellies", as Ezra Pound fumed in his poem *Hugh Selwyn Mauberley* (1920): "There died a myriad ... For an old bitch gone in the teeth, for a botched civilization ..."

Died some, pro patria,
non "dulce" non "et decor" ...
walked eye-deep in hell
believing in old men's lies, then unbelieving
came home, home to a lie,
home to many deceits,
home to old lies and new infamy;
usury old-age and age-thick
and liars in public places.

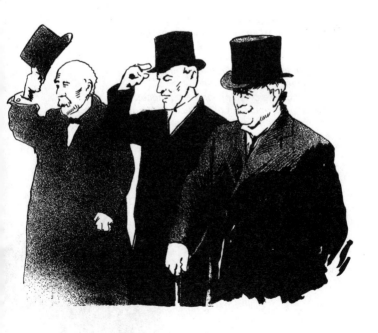

Dulce et decorum est pro patria mori

Heroic patriotism that pre-war schoolboys imbibed from these famous
words of the Roman poet **Horace** (65–8 BC) had become a grotesque
joke for Pound, a sinister lie for the war poet **Wilfred Owen**
(1893–1918), killed in action …

Gas! GAS! Quick, boys!—An ecstasy of fumbling,
Fitting the clumsy helmets just in time,
But someone still was yelling out and stumbling
And floundering like a man in fire or lime.—
Dim through the misty panes and thick green light,
As under a green sea, I saw him drowning.

In all my dreams before my helpless sight
He plunges at me, guttering, choking, drowning.

If in some smothering dreams, you too could pace
Behind the wagon that we flung him in,
And watch the white eyes writhing in his face,
His hanging face, like a devil's sick of sin;
If you could hear, at every jolt, the blood
Come gargling from the froth-corrupted lungs,
Bitter as the cud
Of vile, incurable sores on innocent tongues,—
My friend, you would not tell with such high zest
To children ardent for some desperate glory,
The old Lie: Dulce et decorum est
Pro patria mori.

"And What For?"

The question soon found its answer in two conflicting political remedies. Two decisive events emerged from the "mire and death" of the First World War – the Fascism of Benito Mussolini in 1922, more dangerously aggrandized by Hitler's Nazism; and the Russian Revolution of 1917, co-opted by Lenin's Bolshevik Communism in 1918.

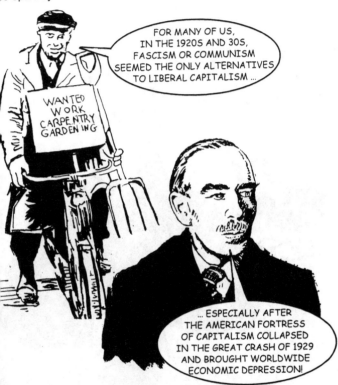

FOR MANY OF US, IN THE 1920S AND 30S, FASCISM OR COMMUNISM SEEMED THE ONLY ALTERNATIVES TO LIBERAL CAPITALISM ...

WANTED WORK CARPENTRY GARDENING

... ESPECIALLY AFTER THE AMERICAN FORTRESS OF CAPITALISM COLLAPSED IN THE GREAT CRASH OF 1929 AND BROUGHT WORLDWIDE ECONOMIC DEPRESSION!

The scenario was in place – a choice of unforeseeable consequences – *either* for the economic recovery of capitalism *or* the triumph of Fascism or that of Communism. Which would it be? Only the renewed carnage, the worse savagery of a Second World War could resolve that – and only *partly*, because it left the US and its allies locked in Cold War conflict with the Communist bloc from 1947 on.

What Would You Choose?

What now seems the "blindness" of these modernists, like Ezra Pound, who took the Fascist route, or many others who embraced Soviet Communism and were destroyed by it, can be better understood by putting ourselves in their shoes. What choice, *then*, would *you* have made? Let's consider the standpoint of the Marxist playwright Bertolt Brecht ...

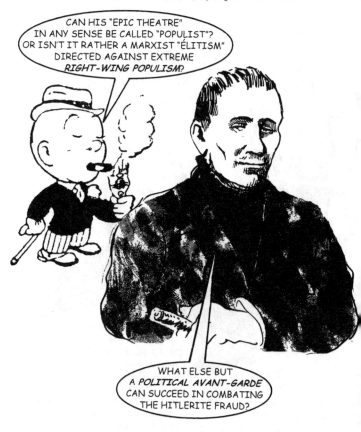

CAN HIS "EPIC THEATRE" IN ANY SENSE BE CALLED "POPULIST"? OR ISN'T IT RATHER A MARXIST "ÉLITISM" DIRECTED AGAINST EXTREME *RIGHT-WING POPULISM?*

WHAT ELSE BUT A *POLITICAL AVANT-GARDE* CAN SUCCEED IN COMBATING THE HITLERITE FRAUD?

Some believe that modernism declined into pessimism in the 1930s. It more likely suffered from a dangerously heady optimism.

Crimes Against Humanity

Any possible euphoria or clear remedy ended with the Second World War. A terrifying catalogue of inhumanity incriminated all sides in the conflict – the Holocaust inflicted by Nazism compares with the many millions destroyed by Stalinism; and the Allies too were guilty of napalming Dresden, A-bombing Japan and other war crimes.

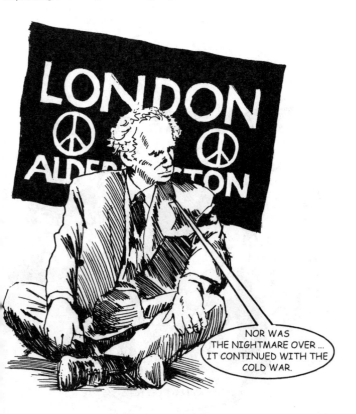

NOR WAS THE NIGHTMARE OVER ... IT CONTINUED WITH THE COLD WAR.

From the late 1940s virtually until the collapse of Communism in 1989, the world endured the psychosis of impending nuclear annihilation in all those gridlock years of undeclared or "cold" war between the USA (and its Western allies) and the Soviet Union (and its Eastern bloc).

Modernism Emigrates to America

Modernism undergoes a relocation to the USA in its third and last phase. The centre of the avant-garde shifts from Paris to New York in the late 1940s and 50s, but the connection had been established much earlier. Alfred Stieglitz's *291* gallery exhibited modern art in 1908. The real turning-point was the famous Armory Show of 1913 which introduced major European modernists to the US, Picasso among them, and Marcel Duchamp, a key figure who settled in New York after 1915.

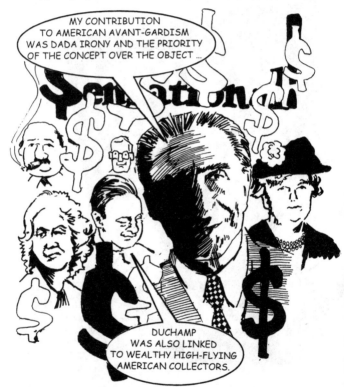

MY CONTRIBUTION TO AMERICAN AVANT-GARDISM WAS DADA IRONY AND THE PRIORITY OF THE CONCEPT OVER THE OBJECT ...

DUCHAMP WAS ALSO LINKED TO WEALTHY HIGH-FLYING AMERICAN COLLECTORS.

The show attracted large crowds in New York, Chicago and Boston, and sold to American collectors. The nucleus of such collections would form MoMA (the Museum of Modern Art in New York) in 1929, one of the most prestigious in the world.

Is America the Natural Home of Modernism?

You would think so. No other country in the world can match America for its vast modernizing energy, its endless appetite for the new. Modernity was built into its revolutionary Declaration of Independence and Constitution. The sprawling free verse of **Walt Whitman** (1819–92) is already a broadcast manifesto of modernism …

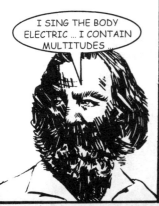

I SING THE BODY ELECTRIC … I CONTAIN MULTITUDES …

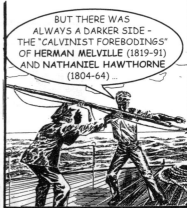

BUT THERE WAS ALWAYS A DARKER SIDE – THE "CALVINIST FOREBODINGS" OF **HERMAN MELVILLE** (1819–91) AND **NATHANIEL HAWTHORNE** (1804-64) …

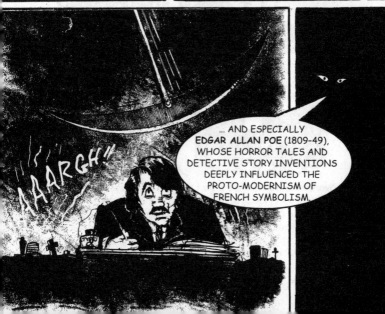

AAARGH!!

… AND ESPECIALLY **EDGAR ALLAN POE** (1809-49), WHOSE HORROR TALES AND DETECTIVE STORY INVENTIONS DEEPLY INFLUENCED THE PROTO-MODERNISM OF FRENCH SYMBOLISM.

The Great Crash and Recovery Programme

America's boundless optimism reached its apogee in the "roaring 20s" – booze, jazz and fabulous wealth on the stock market – and came tumbling down in the great "crash" of 1929. Wall Street financiers jumped from their windows, banks closed, and a grisly economic depression spread across the US and the world.

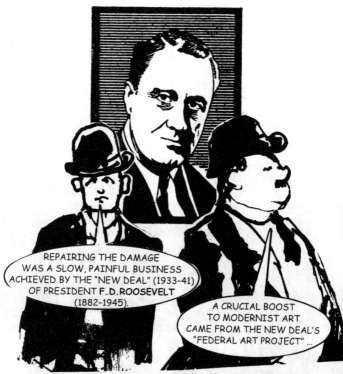

REPAIRING THE DAMAGE WAS A SLOW, PAINFUL BUSINESS ACHIEVED BY THE "NEW DEAL" (1933-41) OF PRESIDENT **F.D.ROOSEVELT** (1882-1945).

A CRUCIAL BOOST TO MODERNIST ART CAME FROM THE NEW DEAL'S "FEDERAL ART PROJECT" ...

Government organized support for art through the Works Progress Administration (1933) and the Federal Art Project (1935). Although the "WPA" style of public art was often uninspired – comparable to "Socialist Realism" in the Soviet Union – the project encouraged those soon to be the stars of avant-gardism: Arshile Gorky, Willem de Kooning, Jackson Pollock and Mark Rothko.

Modernism: the Un-American Activity

"New Deal"-ism was hateful "socialism" in the eyes of American conservatives. And as for modernism – well, that was plainly "un-American"! Here's a quote from a 1949 speech to Congress by Senator for Michigan **George Dondero** (1883–1968), entitled "Modern Art Shackled to Communism" …

The art of the isms, the weapon of the Russian Revolution, is the art which has been transplanted to America … So-called modern or contemporary art in our own beloved country contains all the isms of depravity, decadence, and destruction …

Cubism aims to destroy by designed disorder.
Futurism aims to destroy by the machine myth.
Dadaism aims to destroy by ridicule.
Expressionism aims to destroy by aping the primitive and insane …
Abstractionism aims to destroy by the creation of brainstorms.
Surrealism aims to destroy by the denial of reason …

… The question is, what have we, the plain American people, done to deserve this sore affliction that has been visited upon us so direly; who has brought down this curse upon us; who has let into our homeland this horde of germ-carrying art vermin?

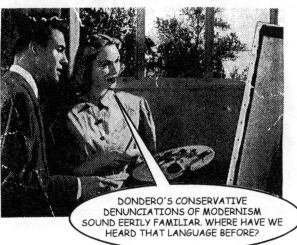

DONDERO'S CONSERVATIVE DENUNCIATIONS OF MODERNISM SOUND EERILY FAMILIAR. WHERE HAVE WE HEARD THAT LANGUAGE BEFORE?

Entartete Kunst

In 1937, Hitler's propagandists organized the most comprehensive showing of modern art – *Entartete Kunst* or "Degenerate Art" – an exhibition which hijacked Nordau's psychiatric diagnosis of degeneracy (see p. 76) for the purpose of "purifying the German race of filth".

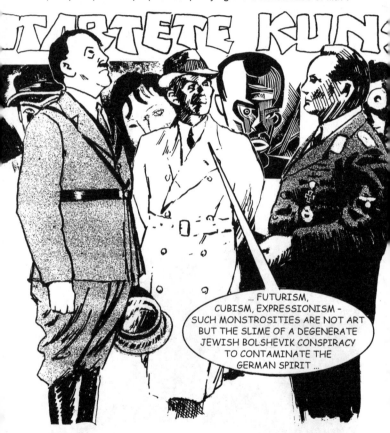

The exhibition was cunningly orchestrated to expose modernism as the "sick, unskilled gibberish of the insane" (but we should note how posters advertising it exploited modernist techniques!).

Soviet Censorship

Nazism's ban on modernism coincides with a similar prohibition in Communist Russia. Avant-garde experimentalism was condemned as a "tool of decadent bourgeois capitalism" and officially declared "terminated" in 1934 by Stalin's dreaded cultural commissar **Andrei Zhdanov** (1896–1948). Henceforth, the orthodox creed of Soviet writers, artists and musicians as "engineers of the human soul" must be **Socialist Realism**. Vladimir Kemenov reiterated this "ideal" in 1947 …

As opposed to decadent bourgeois art, divorced from the people, hostile to the interests of the democratic masses, permeated with biological individualism and mysticism, reactionary and anti-popular, Soviet artists present an art created for the people, inspired by the thoughts, feelings and achievements of the people …

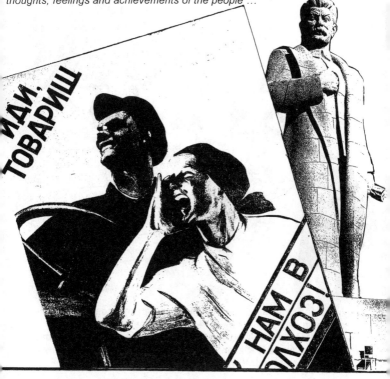

An Unholy Alliance

Senator **Joe McCarthy** (1908–57) terrorized American intellectuals and artists in the early 1950s with his anti-Communist witch-hunts (Senate investigations into "Un-American Activities"). Dondero represents this Cold War "McCarthyite" opposition to modernism, which saw it as a Communist plot to subvert American democracy. His attack echoes that of Nazism and, bizarrely, apes the language of Soviet orthodoxy! What's going on?

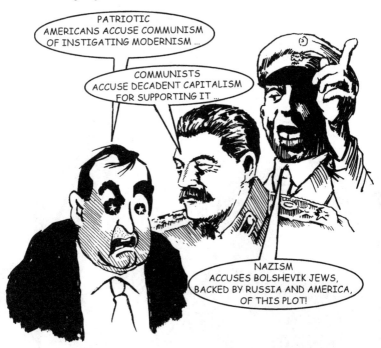

PATRIOTIC AMERICANS ACCUSE COMMUNISM OF INSTIGATING MODERNISM ...

COMMUNISTS ACCUSE DECADENT CAPITALISM FOR SUPPORTING IT ...

NAZISM ACCUSES BOLSHEVIK JEWS, BACKED BY RUSSIA AND AMERICA, OF THIS PLOT!

Apparently they all share a common hostility to modernism, while accusing each other of being responsible for the modernist "conspiracy". How to explain it? Strip away the rhetoric and what's left is an agreement that avant-garde modernism does not serve the needs of **mass popular culture**.

The Elite Defence of Modernism

The counter-attack to McCarthyite populism came from the liberal business wing of the American establishment and those intellectuals who made the case that avant-garde abstract art expresses precisely the freedom denied by the totalitarian Nazi and Stalinist regimes which enforce repressive pseudo-populist culture.

Alfred H. Barr (1902–81), first director of the MoMA, led this argument in 1936 – and produced a famous diagram to confirm his view that abstract art was a rational necessity of progress.

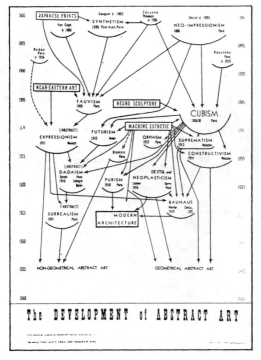

After the Nazis' defeat, Barr focussed on the battle against Communism and McCarthyism as both equally enemies of liberal freedom. "Those who assert or imply that modern art is a subversive instrument of the Kremlin are guilty of fantastic falsehood." (1952)

Kitsch, High Culture and Abstract Expressionism

The art critic **Clement Greenberg** (1909–94) was the High Priest of late modernism. With justice, he might be called the American equivalent of T.W. Adorno. Greenberg's ideas spring from immigrant Jewish socialism, "free-thinking" Marxism and the aesthetics of **Immanuel Kant** (1724–1804). In his seminal anti-capitalist essay "Avant-Garde and Kitsch" (1939), he defined High Culture (reflexive, critical and demanding) against Kitsch (easy enjoyment and passive consumption). Avant-garde methods enable culture to progress – an idea that led him to defend "abstract purism".

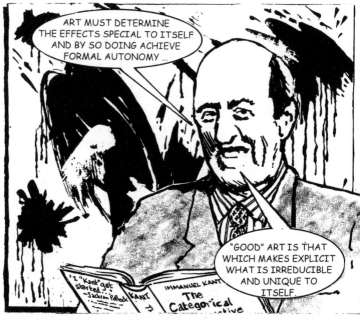

Greenberg's championship of Abstract Expressionism – the paintings of **Jackson Pollock** (1912–56), **Willem de Kooning** (1904–97), **Mark Rothko** (1903–70) and others – was instrumental in securing the Americanization of modernist aesthetic identity. However, a "de-politicization" of his theory was inevitable in the climate of McCarthyite anti-Communism.

Hijacking Abstract Expressionism

Abstract Expressionism achieved its international success in the Cold War 1950s not solely on the aesthetic grounds argued by Greenberg but because of the ideological uses to which it was put. There is evidence of CIA involvement in hijacking this "brain-child" of the liberal establishment for the purpose of opposing Eastern bloc Communism.

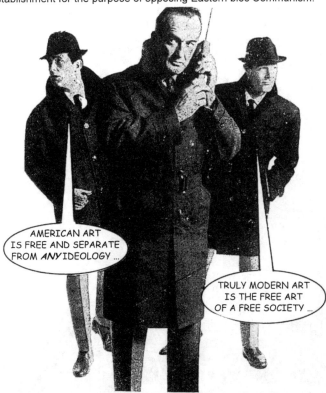

Free, that is, to consume by right of equality. Jackson Pollock's "drip" paintings, along with the latest model Buick, Bendix washing-machine and Lucky Strike cigarettes were equated as symbols of the Great American Dream. Indeed, the influx of European intellectual refugees from Nazism in the 1930s had greatly enhanced the image of America, "fortress of liberty".

Duchamp Descending a Staircase ...

Marcel Duchamp was not a European refugee but an artist who chose neutral America in wartime 1915. His choice makes him a key figure to American modernism – first, as "transatlantic bridge" allying Paris to New York avant-gardism; second, as transition to postmodernism. Duchamp never fully identified with any of the "isms". *Nude Descending a Staircase* of 1912 might look like a Cubist painting, but, in fact, it was a step towards his "mecanthropomorphism" ...

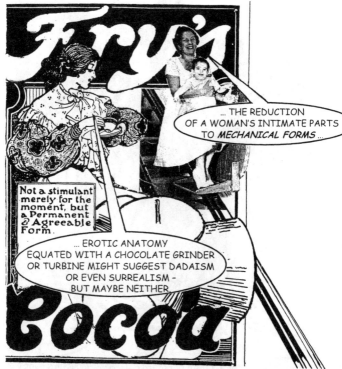

Duchamp's aim was to abandon "retinal painting" and substitute mass-produced, machine-made objects for handmade works of art. After his master-work, *The Large Glass* or *The Bride stripped bare by her bachelors, even* (1915–23), he pretended to abandon art for the "mechanistic sculpture" of chess-playing.

Pop Art or Neo-Dadaism?

Duchamp, as Europeans so often do, had misjudged America and was offended by the entry of "neo-Dadaist" Pop Art in the later 1950s. In 1962, he protested bitterly against Pop Art assemblages of consumer society readymades.

*This neo-Dada which they call New Realism, Pop Art, Assemblage, etc., is an easy way out, and lives on what Dada did. When I discovered readymades, I thought to discourage aesthetics. In neo-Dada they have taken my readymades and found aesthetic beauty in them. I threw the "bottle rack" and the "urinal" into their face as a challenge, and now they admire them for their aesthetic **beauty**!*

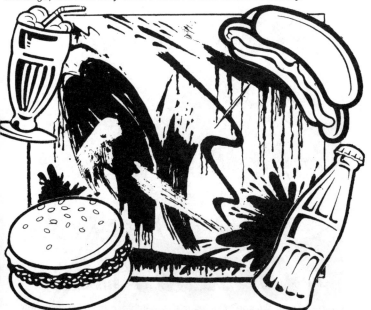

There is a great irony here. Greenberg had defended an "authentic" avant-garde (Cubism, Abstract Expressionism) against a "popular" one that he pejoratively named the "avant-gardism" of Dada and, yes, Duchamp. Greenberg's "purism" was meant to safeguard art from its own dissolution in consumerist capitalism – a desperate attempt that paradoxically helped to make American "pop culture" more secure.

The "End" of Modernism?

From a 1963 interview with the King of Pop Art, **Andy Warhol**
(1903–87) …

*Someone said that Brecht wanted everybody to think alike. I want
everybody to think alike. But Brecht wanted to do it through
Communism, in a way. Russia is doing it under government. It's
happening here all by itself without being under a strict government …
Everybody looks alike and acts alike, and we're getting more and more
that way.*
I think everybody should be a machine.
I think everybody should like everybody.

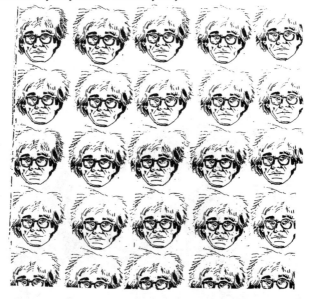

Warhol is right, isn't he? Duchamp's mecanthropomorphism is simply
machine-likeness. Modernism (like Marxism) wanted to go "deep"; but
all that matters is **surface**. What you see is what you get. Meaning is
read from signs that are artificially constructed – and this brings us into
the sphere of postmodernism, of Barthes, Baudrillard, Derrida. "New" in
the USA is an everyday routine, it instantly ages and ends up in the
junk-yard for pastiche recycling.

What is the Relation of Cinema to Modernism?

This postmodern "surface", Warhol himself admits, came from a staple diet of Hollywood cinema and its "dream factory" assemblies of pop icons, Marilyn Monroe, Liz Taylor and all the rest. Should we then acknowledge **film** as the bridge from modernism to postmodernism?

Cinema is the representative mass medium, the "7th art", the very essence of modernity. But does its mass appeal chime with modernism? Modernism subverted "realism" in all sectors of art – novels, poetry, painting, even music. In so doing, it made art more opaque and difficult and thus restricted its appeal. The dominant commercial paradigm of Hollywood cinema did exactly the opposite ...

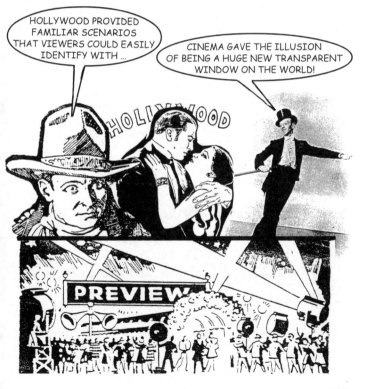

Against the Modernist Grain

Cinema is, in a sense, the fly in the modernist ointment. For the most part, the output from the commercial sector went against the grain of the modernist aesthetic. Hollywood has a bad record of *usefully* employing the creative talents of modernist artists, writers and its more adventurous film directors.

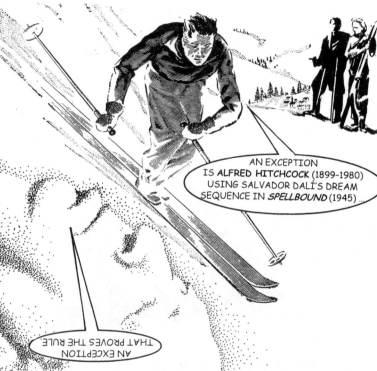

AN EXCEPTION IS **ALFRED HITCHCOCK** (1899-1980) USING SALVADOR DALÍ'S DREAM SEQUENCE IN *SPELLBOUND* (1945)

AN EXCEPTION THAT PROVES THE RULE

The films of **Erich von Stroheim** (1885–1957) were butchered. Eisenstein's visit to Hollywood came to nothing. Renoir's American films were insipid. Bertolt Brecht was only involved in minimal script-writing, so too F. Scott Fitzgerald and other "name" writers who trod the studio treadmills. Later, again, Jean-Paul Sartre's script on Freud to be filmed by **John Huston** (1906–87) was rejected. Etc., etc.

European Art Cinema

One important alternative to Hollywood has been European "art cinema" driven by the imperatives of national cultural identity. It is also known as *auteur* cinema because the director's presence as the film's "author" is strongly forefronted. Perhaps the classic *auteur* film-maker is **Jean Renoir** (1894–79), son of the Impressionist painter **Auguste Renoir** (1841–1919), who shares in his father's amiable *joie de vivre*.

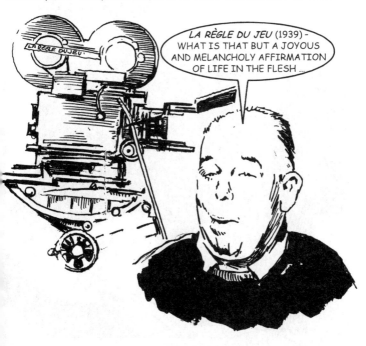

LA RÈGLE DU JEU (1939) – WHAT IS THAT BUT A JOYOUS AND MELANCHOLY AFFIRMATION OF LIFE IN THE FLESH ...

Others in this French school include **René Clair** (1898–1981), who celebrates a whimsical socialism, and **Marcel Carné** (1900–96); in Germany, **Georg Pabst** (1885–1967) and **Ernst Lubitsch** (1892–1947), and many others who employed a sophisticated "authorial" approach to film. In a more ascetic modernist vein, we can name **Carl Dreyer** (1889–1968) and **Robert Bresson** (1907–2000), but these film artists too remain within a popular mainstream.

Avant-garde Cinema: Surrealism

Another alternative to dominant cinema is avant-garde film-making, often defined as "pure" modernist films, such as Buñuel and Dalí's Surrealist ones (see p. 91), because they display similar formal avant-garde qualities to those operative in other arts.

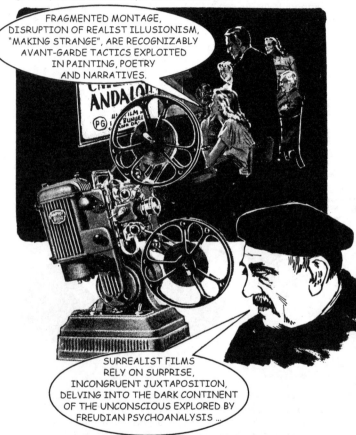

FRAGMENTED MONTAGE, DISRUPTION OF REALIST ILLUSIONISM, "MAKING STRANGE", ARE RECOGNIZABLY AVANT-GARDE TACTICS EXPLOITED IN PAINTING, POETRY AND NARRATIVES.

SURREALIST FILMS RELY ON SURPRISE, INCONGRUENT JUXTAPOSITION, DELVING INTO THE DARK CONTINENT OF THE UNCONSCIOUS EXPLORED BY FREUDIAN PSYCHOANALYSIS ...

The iconography and sexual sub-text of films like *Un Chien Andalou* are connected to Surrealist paintings and poetry, not only in this case because Dalí was primarily a painter, but in many other instances.

Expressionism in Films

German films such as Robert Wiene's sinister madhouse *Cabinet of Dr Caligari* (1920), F.W. Murnau's vampire *Nosferatu* (1922), Fritz Lang's insane master criminal *Dr Mabuse, the Gambler* (1922) and others were modelled on Expressionist painting, theatre, poetry and stock German "Gothic horror" fiction. "Films must be drawings brought to life", asserted the scenic designer of *Caligari*. But these films concealed an explosive problem.

EXPRESSIONIST ART WAS BEING DOWNGRADED TO FILM VERSIONS OF "SICK BRAINS" ...

... AN INEVITABLE STEP TOWARDS HITLER'S VIEW ON "DEGENERATE ART"!

Siegfried Kracauer's classic study, *From Caligari to Hitler* (1947), traces Expressionist film-making in its relation to the German film industry Ufa (Universum Film A.G.) from its foundation in 1917, for the purpose of wartime propaganda, to the Nazi takeover.

Avant-garde Soviet Films

While the German film industry slipped dangerously towards Nazism, the avant-garde situation in the Soviet Union, at least in its infancy, was very different. The 1918 October Revolution (headed by a small political élite) occurred in a setting of already established avant-gardism (headed by a small aesthetic élite). For a time, the two energies seemed to combine – experimental modernism *was* the art of the revolution, as conveyed by Malevich's Suprematism, Tatlin's Constructivism, Mayakovsky's Futurist poetry and so on – apparently.

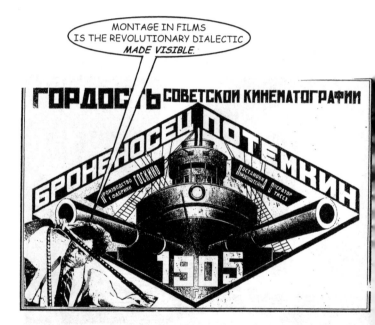

MONTAGE IN FILMS IS THE REVOLUTIONARY DIALECTIC *MADE VISIBLE*.

The master *auteur* of early Soviet film was without doubt Sergei Eisenstein in works like *Battleship Potemkin* (1925). Dziga Vertov's *The Man With a Movie Camera* (1929), a film of daring self-reflexivity, explored the nature of cinematic vision by literally focussing on the frames that make up the moving image. Experimentalism ended in 1932 with Zhdanovite "Socialist Realism", the dissolution of all existing art groups and their replacement by the state-controlled Artists' Union.

Later 1960s avant-garde film-making – agit-prop, underground and other coterie groups – accounts for a tiny fraction of film production on a global scale. It does not represent *cinema*. The real challenge is to think of mainstream cinema as being *inextricably* part of the modernist project. **André Malraux** (1901–76), writer, politician, and himself producer of a fine independent film, grasped the issue perfectly.

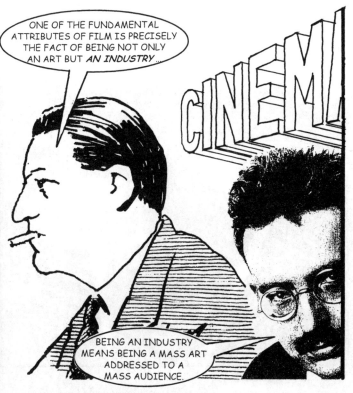

ONE OF THE FUNDAMENTAL ATTRIBUTES OF FILM IS PRECISELY THE FACT OF BEING NOT ONLY AN ART BUT *AN INDUSTRY* ...

BEING AN INDUSTRY MEANS BEING A MASS ART ADDRESSED TO A MASS AUDIENCE.

One of the key texts of modernism, Walter Benjamin's essay, "The Work of Art in the Age of Mechanical Reproduction" (1936), championed film and the reproducible media because they dispensed with the "aura" of traditional art and thus encouraged a more democratic, politically engaged practice. Mass culture will mean *more* but not necessarily *worse* culture.

Reconsidering Hollywood

It is too easy to castigate Hollywood merely as the purveyor of shallow illusions, driven exclusively by commercial imperatives and profit. Hollywood is also capable of seizing popular fantasies and magically transforming them into strong collective images and stories. The experience of some "modernist" directors and artists crushed by the commercial Hollywood machine is counter-balanced by the example of other *emigré* directors from Nazi Germany – Fritz Lang, **Douglas Sirk** (1900–87), **Max Ophuls** (1902–57), **Joseph von Sternberg** (1894–1969), **Billy Wilder** (b. 1906) and many others.

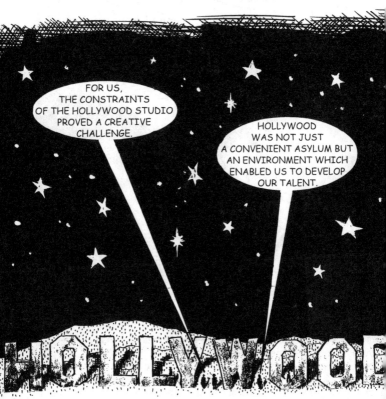

Consider these examples of Hollywood's industrial output – the melodramas of Ophuls' *Letter From an Unknown Woman* (1948) or Sirk's *Magnificent Obsession* (1953), Lang's thriller *The Big Heat* (1953), the comedies of Billy Wilder, such as *Some Like it Hot* (1959), or the baroque extravaganzas of von Sternberg: *Shanghai Express* (1932) and *The Scarlet Empress* (1934).

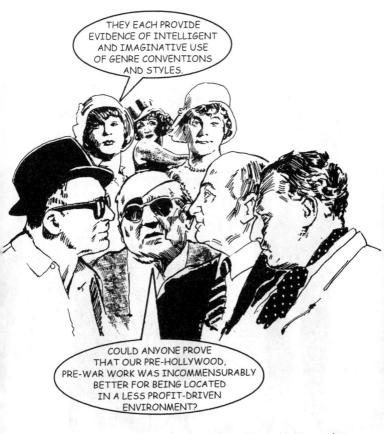

The same ability to be inventive with – as opposed to against – popular and mass forms of entertainment informs a whole body of Hollywood film-makers, not just the European *emigré* directors.

The New Wave

Jean-Luc Godard (b. 1930), **François Truffaut** (1932–84), **Jacques Rivette** (b. 1928), **Claude Chabrol** (b. 1930), **Eric Rohmer** (b. 1920) and others became the film-makers of the French "New Wave" (*Nouvelle Vague*) in the late 1950s. They began as critics and cinephiles who first recognized the extraordinary Hollywood paradox.

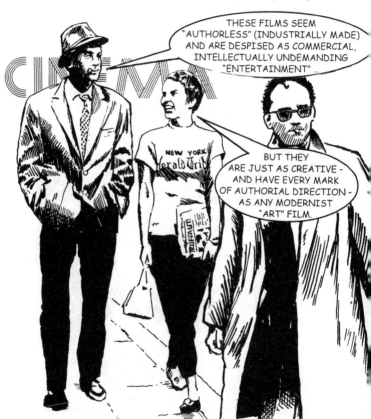

THESE FILMS SEEM "AUTHORLESS" (INDUSTRIALLY MADE) AND ARE DESPISED AS *COMMERCIAL*, INTELLECTUALLY UNDEMANDING "ENTERTAINMENT"...

BUT THEY ARE JUST AS CREATIVE – AND HAVE EVERY MARK OF AUTHORIAL DIRECTION – AS ANY MODERNIST "ART" FILM.

Jean-Luc Godard is the exemplary figure who, rather like Marcel Duchamp in art, sets in crisis the accepted ways of film-making and charts the passage from modernism to postmodernism.

Breathless …

Godard's *A Bout de souffle* (*Breathless*, 1960) paid homage to American "B" pictures but was modernist in fragmenting its narrative. *Pierrot le fou* (1965), quirkier and pastiche-like, edges out of modernism. *Week-end* (1967) and *Wind From the East* (1969) explode the whole avant-garde business. His hard-core political films of the late 1960s and 70s seem to regress to agit-prop tactics …

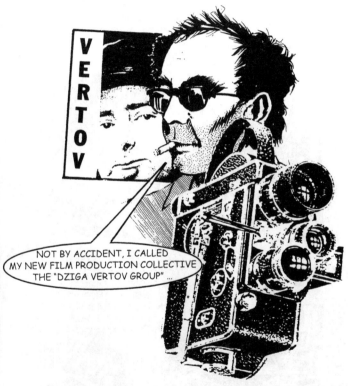

He enters postmodern territory with *Tout va bien* (1972), in its mix of self-reflexivity and superstars (Jane Fonda, Yves Montand). Encounters with video and the ongoing story *Histoire(s) du cinéma* (1989–2000) might either be a lament for the "death" of cinema or a celebration of the endless begetting of histories by new technologies.

New Technologies = Postmodernism?

Godard's interest in video gives us another clue. Are we wrong to think of cinema as the "bridge" to postmodernism? Shouldn't we instead look to television, video, the digital revolution, the Internet – an entire new world of "telematics"? We've seen the *past* technologies which underpinned modernity and modernism's reactions to them, but what's happening *now*, in the present?

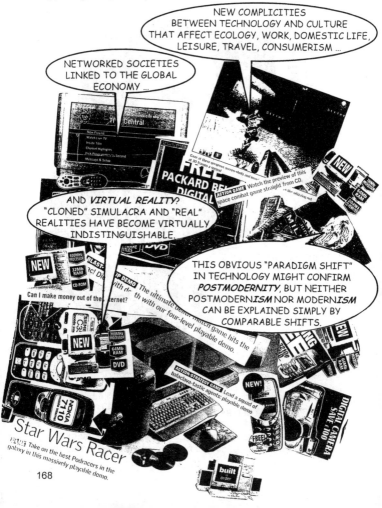

NEW COMPLICITIES BETWEEN TECHNOLOGY AND CULTURE THAT AFFECT ECOLOGY, WORK, DOMESTIC LIFE, LEISURE, TRAVEL, CONSUMERISM ...

NETWORKED SOCIETIES LINKED TO THE GLOBAL ECONOMY ...

AND *VIRTUAL REALITY*? "CLONED" SIMULACRA AND "REAL" REALITIES HAVE BECOME VIRTUALLY INDISTINGUISHABLE.

THIS OBVIOUS "PARADIGM SHIFT" IN TECHNOLOGY MIGHT CONFIRM *POSTMODERNITY*, BUT NEITHER POSTMODERN*ISM* NOR MODERN*ISM* CAN BE EXPLAINED SIMPLY BY COMPARABLE SHIFTS.

Has Modernism "Ended"?

Being "modern" can have no imaginable end. Can we become "more" modern? "Ultra"-modern? "Supra"-modern? Or "less-modern"? What's more modern than modern?

But, strictly speaking, to be "post"-modern doesn't make any sense.

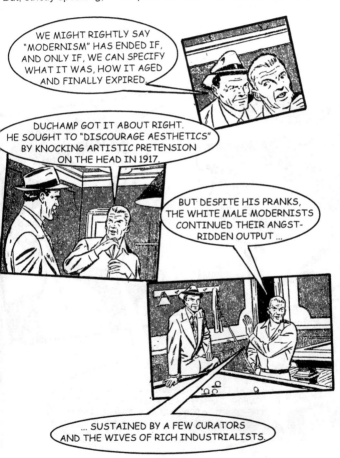

WE MIGHT RIGHTLY SAY "MODERNISM" HAS ENDED IF, AND ONLY IF, WE CAN SPECIFY WHAT IT WAS, HOW IT AGED AND FINALLY EXPIRED.

DUCHAMP GOT IT ABOUT RIGHT. HE SOUGHT TO "DISCOURAGE AESTHETICS" BY KNOCKING ARTISTIC PRETENSION ON THE HEAD IN 1917.

BUT DESPITE HIS PRANKS, THE WHITE MALE MODERNISTS CONTINUED THEIR ANGST-RIDDEN OUTPUT ...

... SUSTAINED BY A FEW CURATORS AND THE WIVES OF RICH INDUSTRIALISTS.

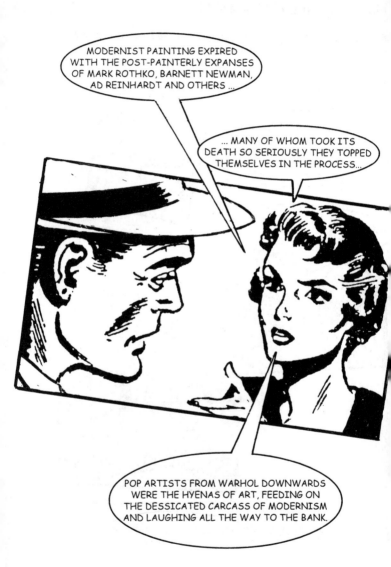

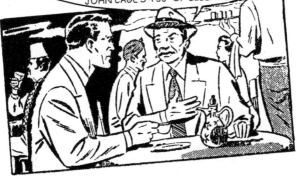

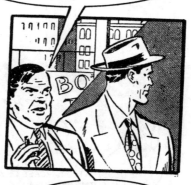

* 4' 33" (1952)

Postmodern MoMA

Irony of ironies! A largely discredited modernist architecture finds its last validation in sheltering the relics of "great works" of modern art, fetishes invested with all the "aura" that Benjamin thought would vanish. New York's Museum of Modern Art (MoMA), the Guggenheim Museum, the Pompidou Centre, the Bilbao Guggenheim, are themselves relics of a bygone utopian project announced by Le Corbusier in 1923. The millennium Tate Modern, lodged in **Gilbert Scott**'s (1880–1960) defunct power station on London's Thames Bankside, is the best example yet of functionalist modern architecture put to dysfunctional service. Its giant chimney raises spectres of a crematorium ...

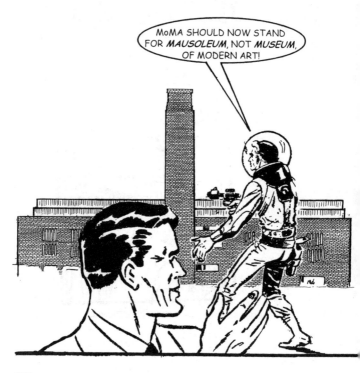

Out of Babylon

But perhaps it was inevitable that modernism would be reconfigured by the next "postmodern" phase of modernity. In other words, modernism hasn't "ended" so much as become *imbedded* in the ongoing programme of modernity, itself a project without an end. We can look at postmodernism in two ways …

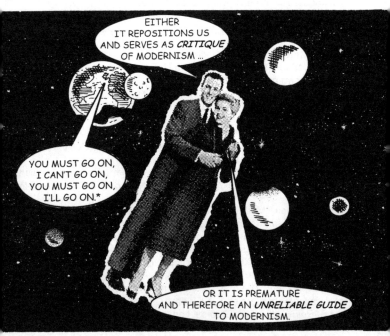

These are not contradictory but complementary ways of thinking about our present situation, reminders that we should reflect again on the complexities that modernism faced in the relations of ethics to aesthetics, politics to style, high culture to mass culture, innovation to tradition, and all the issues still urgently relevant to us. We can never start from zero – and modernism is a present resource.

Modernism's origins, like its "endings", remain elusive, open to speculation, controversy and **retrieval**.

* *The Unnamable* Samuel Beckett (1953)

Bibliography

The following very selective bibliography is just one biased and personalized route through an embarrassment of secondary literature riches.

Benjamin, Walter, *Illuminations*, London: Pimlico, 1999. Every postmodernist home should possess a copy.

Berman, Marshall, *All that is Solid Melts into Air: The Experience of Modernity*, London: Verso, 1983. An exuberantly politicized take on modernity.

Butler, Christopher, *Early Modernism: Literature, Music and Painting in Europe, 1900–1916*, Oxford: Oxford University Press, 1994. A useful multi-art form perspective.

Clark, T.J., *Farewell to an Idea: Episodes from a History of Modernism*, New Haven and London: Yale University Press, 1999. From one of the foremost art historians of the modernist movement.

Conrad, Peter, *Modern Times, Modern Places*, London: Thames and Hudson, 1998. A very readable and engaging account, full of intricate connections, entry and exit points.

Cook, Pam, and Bernink, Mieke (eds), *The Cinema Book*, 2nd edition, London: BFI, 1999. An excellent introduction to different aspects of film study.

Crow, Thomas, "Modernism and Mass Culture in the Visual Arts", in *Modern Art in the Common Culture*, New Haven CN: Yale University Press, 1996. A key intervention in the mass culture and art debate.

Donald, James, *Imagining the Modern City*, Minneapolis: University of Minnesota Press, 1999. A fascinating exploration of the politics and poetics of the modern city.

Hansen, Miriam, "The mass production of the senses: classical cinema as vernacular modernism", in Gledhill, Christine, and Williams, Linda (eds), *Reinventing Film Studies*, London: Arnold, 2000. A stimulating analysis of the problematic relationship of film to modernism.

Huyssen, Andreas, *After the Great Divide: Modernism, Mass Culture, Postmodernism*, Bloomington and Indianapolis: Indiana University Press, 1986. A thought-provoking account of the connections between modernism and postmodernism.

Marvin, Carolyn, *When Old Technologies were New: thinking about electric communication in the late nineteenth century*, New York and Oxford: Oxford University Press, 1988. Provides an invaluable "archaeological" context for understanding modern technology and culture.

Moretti, Franco, *Signs Taken for Wonders: Essays in the Sociology of Literary Forms*, London: Verso, 1983. An original and productive series of interpretations and readings of modernist cultural phenomena.

Nicholls, Peter, *Modernisms: A Literary Guide*, London: Macmillan, 1995. One of the best overall literary guides and introductions.

Sparke, Penny, *A Century of Design: Design Pioneers of the Twentieth Century*, London: Mitchell Beazley, 1998. A very good survey of modern design.

Willett, John, *The New Sobriety: Art and Politics in the Weimar Period 1917–33*, London: Thames and Hudson, 1978. An accessible verbal and visual narrative of one of the high moments of modernism.

Williams, Raymond, *The Politics of Modernism: Against the New Conformists*, London: Verso, 1989. Contains some lucid essays on the relationship of modernism and the avant-garde to politics.

Wollen, Peter, "The Two Avant-Gardes", in *Readings and Writings: Semiotic Counter-Strategies*, London: Verso, 1982. A polemical and historical account of parallel film movements.

Some useful anthologies:

Chipp, Herschel B. (ed.), *Theories of Modern Art*, Berkeley and London: University of California Press, 1968.

Frascina, Francis, and Harrison, Charles (eds), *Modern Art and Modernism: a Critical Anthology*, London: Paul Chapman, 1982.

Harrison, Charles, and Wood, Paul (eds), *Art in Theory, 1900–1990: an Anthology of Changing Ideas*, Oxford: Blackwell, 1992.

Levenson, Michael (ed.), *The Cambridge Companion to Modernism*, Cambridge: Cambridge University Press, 1999.

Among a plethora of journals, *Modernism/Modernity* is recommended.

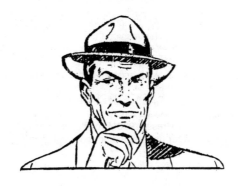

Index